Chas H Moore

THE ANALYSED BIBLE

THE GOSPEL ACCORDING TO MATTHEW

THE GOSPEL ACCORDING TO MATTHEW

BY THE REV.
G. CAMPBELL MORGAN, D.D.

HODDER AND STOUGHTON
LONDON NEW YORK TORONTO

THE GOSPEL ACCORDING
TO MATTHEW

BY

G. CAMPBELL MORGAN, D.D.

HODDER AND STOUGHTON

Printed by Hazell, Watson & Viney, Ld., London and Aylesbury.

PREFACE

THE Preface to this Volume is found in the Chapter on Matthew, in Volume III. of "The Analysed Bible."

Herein we proceed at once to the more detailed analysis of what is set forth in bare outline therein.

Familiarity with that outline is necessary to the study of this book.

G. CAMPBELL MORGAN.

PREFACE

THE Preface to this Volume is found
in the Chapter on Matthew, in
Volume III. of " The Analysed Bible ".
Herein we proceed at once to the more
detailed analysis of what is set forth in
bare outline therein.
Familiarity with that outline is necessary
to the study of this book.

G. CAMPBELL MORGAN.

CONTENTS

HIS PERSON

Contents

Contents

Contents

HIS PASSION

x

Contents

Contents

MATTHEW

A. HIS PERSON

THE Gospel according to Matthew presents Jesus of Nazareth as the Hebrew Messiah, but not according to the narrow interpretation of Messiahship which characterised the age of Hebrew failure. He is presented as the King of the chosen people, and the Saviour of the World.

The first division of the Gospel is characterised by the carefulness with which Matthew presents the Person of the King in the essential matters of His relationship to earth, to heaven, and to hell. There is an absence of detail in the story of the first thirty years in the life of Jesus, those matters only being considered which deal with these relationships.

I. HIS RELATION TO EARTH

His relation to earth is revealed by the

3

genealogy, the story of His birth, and the account of the work of the herald.

i. THE GENEALOGY

The section containing the genealogy consists of the title, the tables, and the summary.

a. THE TITLE

The form in which the title is written graphically sets before the mind the relation of the Person of the King to the history of the ancient people of God, as it declares Him to be of the royal line, son of David ; and of the chosen seed, son of Abraham.

b. THE TABLES

The first table traces the relation of David to Abraham. Beginning with the founder and father of the nation, it moves forward along the line of elect succession toward the Person of the King in Whom the Divine ideal was most perfectly exemplified in the history of the nation. The principle of election is revealed in the

4

declaration that Isaac begat Jacob, there
being no reference to Esau; and that while
the other sons of Jacob are referred to,
Judah being the father of the tribe pre-
destined to royalty, is particularly named.

The irregularities of this first table are
in themselves instructive. They consist of
the reference to the fact that Judah begat
Zerah of Tamar; that Boaz was a de-
scendant of Rahab; and that the mother
of Obed was Ruth. None of these things
are really necessary to genealogical accuracy,
but their inclusion reveals the fact that
the principle of election was that of the
operation of grace in answer to faith, as
the incidents suggested by the names will
demonstrate.

The second table traces the relation of
David to Jechoniah, the king of the royal
line who occupied the throne at the time
of the carrying away to Babylon.

Again the irregularities are suggestive,
consisting of the reference, though not by
name, to Bathsheba the mother of Solomon;
the omission of the names of Ahaziah, Joash,

and Amaziah between Joram and Uzziah ; and the omission of the name of Jehoiakim between those of Josiah and Jechoniah. In this case the principle of election is again recognised. In the reference to Bathsheba it is seen triumphing over sin, and yet revealing how the sinful act resulted in the harvest of failure. The omission of the names between Joram and Uzziah is significant in that they are the names of the immediate descendants of the daughter of Ahab and Jezebel. The omission of Jehoiakim is not easy to account for. It may have been the mistake of a copyist, but if he were included, then fifteen generations would be accounted for ; unless the term, "the time of the carrying away to Babylon" referred to the fact that Jehoiakim became tributary to Babylon.

The third table traces the relation of Jechoniah the king who was actually reigning when Judah was carried into captivity, to Joseph the husband of Mary, the mother of the Christ.

The first irregularity in this table consists of the fact, that in order to the completion of the fourteen, Jechoniah must be counted, which he ought not to be, if he is counted in the former table. This adds weight to the view that the name of Jehoiakim ought to occur in the previous one, and that its omission is probably the mistake of a copyist. The final irregularity is that this whole movement of direct succession culminates in Joseph, and Matthew is careful to name him only as the husband of Mary, and not as the father of Jesus. Thus in this particular line of succession, Jesus is only included as the result of the fact that His mother, Mary, was the wife of Joseph. There is practically no question that Mary was of the same royal line, and related by blood to the man whom she married, possibly as cousin.

c. THE SUMMARY

The summary speaks of the three tables as each recording fourteen generations. Its wording must be carefully noted. With regard to the first table the statement is

7

perfectly distinct that " All the generations from Abraham unto David are fourteen." With regard to the second and the third the statement is merely, " From David unto the carrying away to Babylon fourteen generations ; and from the carrying away to Babylon unto the Christ fourteen generations." Not, it will be observed, " all the generations " ; but simply the indication of the fact that fourteen have been named in each of these two tables. Thus the grouping into fourteens is poetic and symbolical, rather than arithmetical and actual. The thought is that of the Kingdom, and the outstanding events are made the crises ; first, Abraham, the beginning of the movement ; then David, the realisation of national life under a king ; then the captivity, the decadence of the nation, and its failure ; and then Jesus, the Messiah, the true King and Restorer of the Divine Order.

ii. THE BIRTH

The birth of the King is dealt with by an account of the discovery of the mystery, and the chronicle of certain events happening in connection therewith.

a. THE DISCOVERY OF THE MYSTERY

With reverent reticence the story of the first consciousness of the awe-inspiring mystery concerning the being of Jesus is recorded. By first consciousness we refer to a consciousness resulting from observation unilluminated by revelation. Of course to Mary the profound secret had been revealed by angel annunciation, but of this Matthew gives no account. To Joseph, her betrothed husband, the consciousness came almost as an assault upon his confidence in Mary. The fine nature of the man is however manifested in the declaration that he was " a righteous man," and did not desire to make her a public example, but "was minded to put her away privily."

This startling consciousness was now

11

explained to him by direct revelation, an angel appearing to him in a dream, and telling him also the profound and awe-inspiring secret which had been revealed to Mary, that the Child begotten in her, was of the Holy Ghost.

The instruction of the angel called Joseph into co-operation, as it told him that he should call the name of the Son Jesus, and declared to him the true meaning of His coming in simplest and sublimest language, in the words, "it is He that shall save His people from their sins."

The angelic messenger proceeded to strengthen his faith and comfort his heart by declaring that all this was in fulfilment of the ancient, mystic prophecy of Isaiah, with which he was undoubtedly familiar.

This interpretation of the prophecy of Isaiah by the angelic messenger stands at the commencement of this Gospel of Matthew as distinct and definite a revelation of the absolute Deity of Jesus as does the mystic prologue of the Gospel according to John.

Again the fine character of Joseph is revealed in the account of his obedience to the angelic revelation. While the story is a brief one, it needs careful reading and close attention, in order that we may appreciate its value. He at once took Mary to be his wife, thus giving her the protection of his love in the period which it is impossible to think of without realising that it was one of suffering and trial, in view of the fact that neighbours and friends were in entire darkness as to the profound work of God which was proceeding in their midst.

His attitude moreover was that of a reverent recognition of the awful sacredness of the life of the woman whom all generations should call blessed.

When at last the Son was born, in obedience to the heavenly vision, and so in co-operation with the will of God, he immediately called His name Jesus.

b. THE COINCIDENT EVENTS

In this section we have the record of two

remarkable events closely connected with the birth of Jesus, those namely of the coming of the wise men ; and the slaughter of the children.

1. *The Coming of the wise Men*

The Kingdom was not ready for the King. Therefore there was no organised reception on the part of those who should have been waiting for Him. That which is pre-eminently remarkable about the coming of these wise men from the East is the fact that they were guided by a star which they had seen. There has been much written concerning these men and this appearance ; but it is impossible to write with any detailed definiteness. One of the most interesting and probable suggestions is that they were Persian Magi, familiar with the ancient prophecy of Balaam, that a star should come out of Jacob, and with the visions and prophecies of Daniel ; and that to these men, waiting in hope amid prevalent darkness, there was granted this definite sign from heaven, guiding them to the place of the new-born King. Their inquiry was marked by great definiteness, as arriving in Jerusalem they said, " Where is He that is born King of the Jews ? for we saw His star in the east, and are come to worship Him."

Such an inquiry inevitably produced a startling effect upon Herod, the Idumæan usurper of the throne, who immediately gathered together a special council of the religious officials and teachers. The demand he made upon them was a very definite one, that they should tell him where the Messiah should be born. Their familiarity with their own prophecies is evidenced by the fact that they immediately replied, In Bethlehem ; and in proof of their declaration, quoted from the prophecy of Micah. Thus informed by the council, Herod held further private conference with the Magi, giving them the information he had obtained, and charging them that when they found Him, they should report to him. That his intention was sinister there can be no doubt, but he veiled that intention by the suggestion that he also desired to worship.

Thus instructed, they went forward, and immediately to their great gladness the star again appeared, and led them to the very spot where the young child lay.

It is a great picture, that of these loyal souls of another nation than the chosen; as, unstaggered by the poverty of His earthly surroundings, they offered Him their choice gifts of gold and frankincense and myrrh. Being warned of God, they did not return to Herod, but departed to their own country.

2. *The Slaughter of the Innocents*

While special heavenly guidance was thus given to the men of another nation, the under-world of evil was moved to its centre by the advent of the Messiah; and found vent through the false king Herod in his slaughter of the innocents. Finding that he had been foiled in his evil purposes, he adopted the inhuman and drastic method of slaying all the male children in Bethlehem and its borders under two years of age ; and the whole region was plunged in desolation and sorrow. Heaven and hell were thus moved at His coming, and those on earth nearest to each, in some way recognised the fact. The great multitudes remained in ignorance.

At the death of Herod, which Josephus tells us took place in the thirty-seventh year of his reign, and the seventieth of his age, an angel again appeared to Joseph, commanding him to take the Child back into the land of Israel. That the sojourn in Egypt was of no lengthy duration is evident from the fact that the angel still referred to Jesus as " the young child." On the return journey, being further warned of God, Joseph returned to Nazareth in Galilee, which for many years was to be the home of Jesus. Matthew's reference to this as fulfilling that which was spoken by the prophets, is interesting. It should be carefully observed that his reference is not to any particular prophecy, but to the general teaching of the prophets. The teaching referred to undoubtedly was that which the nation had never really apprehended, that of His lowliness, and of His relation to despicable situations and peoples. There is no connection between this word Nazarene and Nazarite.

iii. The Herald

The next matter of importance in dealing with the relation of the King to earth is that He should be introduced in His full manhood; and for this appearance we are prepared by the story of the ministry of John the Baptist, His herald. The account of this ministry is a brief one, but its two-fold nature is evident. It was distinctly Hebrew, and definitely Christian; and constituted the link between the two in the economy of God.

a. THE HEBREW MINISTRY

The phrase with which the section opens, "And in those days," has caused some difficulty, and that principally by the attempt to relate it to that which has gone before. As a matter of fact between the return to Nazareth and the appearance of Jesus in connection with the ministry of John, nearly thirty years must have elapsed. It is far more likely therefore that the phrase is one peculiarly that of Matthew, as writing long years afterwards, his mind fixed upon the whole ministry and work of his Lord, and about to recount the story of how it began, he wrote, "In those days."

The early ministry of John was evidently a most remarkable one, and in the simple and true sense of the word, a popular one. The particular symbol which he associated with his preaching was that of baptism. Hence he is called John the Baptist, or more accurately, John the Baptizer; and in this way he was described by Josephus.

The burden of his message is first recorded in the words, "Repent ye; for the Kingdom of heaven is at hand." This is the first occasion of the occurrence of the phrase, the Kingdom of heaven, which from this point is constantly repeated in the course of the narrative. To the ears of the men who heard it as John used it, it was perfectly familiar, and conveyed the central religious idea of their history. However far they had wandered from a correct interpretation of its meaning, they still looked upon themselves as being the peculiar people of God, the theocracy, the Kingdom of heaven. The implication of the message of John was that of their failure to realise the ideal, and the burden of his cry was that they should repent toward that Kingdom ; that is, that they should reconsider, and consequently readjust their lives toward that master principle. There was however, a special significance in his declaration that the Kingdom of heaven was " at hand," suggesting as it did, some approaching event, the nearness of which added urgency to his demand for repentance.

Matthew interpreted that burden by his careful declaration that John was the one who fulfilled the prophecy of Isaiah, in which he had declared that before the advent of Messiah, a voice should be heard proclaiming in the wilderness the advent of Messiah, and calling men to prepare for it.

In one brief paragraph the record gives us a picture of the instrument of this message as he appeared. His manner of life was that of the stern ascetic, withdrawn from the habits and customs of his age ; and appearing only in order to interpret the need of that age, to proclaim the advent of Another, and to call men into the right attitude in which to receive Him.

The effect produced is then declared, and it is evident that it was a most remarkable one ; for vast multitudes of the people crowded out into the wilderness region, and listening to him, yielded to his symbolic rite of baptism, confessing their sins. For a while, at any rate, the whole region was under the spell of his preaching, and men acknowledged the truth of his words of condemnation, and obeyed his call to repentance.

b. THE CHRISTIAN MINISTRY

In the course of the narrative the word " But " is used significantly, " But when he saw many of the Pharisees and Sadducees coming to his baptism." These were the leaders of the people, representing two schools of degenerate religious thinking. The Pharisees had allowed a passion for

the maintenance of the separation of the
Hebrew people from contamination with
other nations, to degenerate into elaborate
ritualism, in which by the multiplication of
forms and ceremonies, they sought to secure
the end they aimed at. The Sadducees
were in direct opposition to the Pharisees,
in that they were rationalists, denying all
the supernatural, and contenting themselves
with a purely material and negative form
of morality.

These leaders were themselves at last
constrained to attend the preaching of this
man, drawn undoubtedly by the influence
he had produced upon the multitudes.
Their coming was the occasion for the
delivery by John of a message which
definitely declared the near advent of the
King Himself.

That message first took the form of the
severest denunciation of these men, as he
described them as an offspring of vipers, and
in evident satire inquired, " Who warned
you to flee from the wrath to come ? "

Seeing however, that they had come, he

uttered to them also the same call to repentance, and at the same time warned
them against any false confidence in their
relation to Abraham.

In immediate connection with these words
addressed to the religious leaders, he uttered
his great proclamation concerning the coming One. The first note of this proclamation was an announcement of judgment as
he said, "Even now is the axe laid unto the
root of the trees." The picture suggested
is not that of an axe being wielded, but that
of the woodman preparing himself for his
work, while the axe which he is to use lies
at the root of the trees among which he
is presently to move in discrimination and
judgment. It was the declaration that an
hour of crisis had arrived, and that all fruit-
less things would be hewn down and cast
into the fire for destruction.

Then leaving the realm of indefinite
illustration, he proclaimed the imminent
advent of Messiah, first announcing His
pre-eminence by declaring that by comparison, his own ministry and he himself

were as nothing, in the presence of the majesty of the One Who was to be revealed, and of the prevailing power of the ministry which He would exercise.

He described that ministry as being re-generative, in that He would baptize with the Holy Ghost and fire ; and restorative, in that He would winnow the threshing-floor with His fan, gathering all precious things into His garner, and destroying the worthless with unquenchable fire.

II. HIS RELATION TO HEAVEN

This is a very brief paragraph, but its importance cannot be over-estimated, affording as it does a key to the whole method of the King in that ministry which is afterwards described in detail in the course of the Gospel. Here at last the King emerged from the seclusion of the life at Nazareth, and the matter of supreme importance is the revelation which this picture affords of His relation to heaven. There are three aspects of the story which demand our attention, those namely of His assumption of responsibility; His anointing for office; and His attestation by God.

i. ASSUMPTION OF RESPONSIBILITY

The coming of Jesus to John is full of interest in two ways; first that it was from Galilee, and secondly that it was for the express purpose of being baptized by John. It was from Galilee, that is, from Nazareth where He had been living during all the years, from the hour in which as a young

Child, He had been taken there by Joseph and Mary. We have no detailed record of the doing of those years, and that fact in itself gives the greater importance to what took place in connection with His baptism, as we shall see presently. It is to be carefully observed that His coming was not that of curiosity, neither was it that of general interest in the ministry of John, but rather that of the set purpose of submitting Himself to the baptism of the great prophet of repentance, and thus of identifying Himself with the people to whom that message had been delivered.

The recognition of this second fact enables us to understand the protest of John, who it is perfectly evident, was familiar with Him. He was conscious that this One Who came among the multitudes, and to all appearance was so much one of them that they did not distinguish Him or recognise that He was any other than one of themselves, was in very deed the King Himself, the mighty One Whose shoe-latchet he was not worthy to unloose His protest however, was supremely a recognition of the purity and power of the Messiah.

John had been preaching the necessity for repentance, and had been baptizing thereunto; but here was One able to baptize into cleansing and life by the Holy Ghost and fire, and John knew his need of that baptism.

To the protest of John, Jesus replied in words full of the profoundest significance. He did not deny what John had said as to his own need of the baptism in the Spirit; but appealed to him in words which indicated His consciousness of purpose and determination to fulfil it; "Suffer it now: for thus it becometh us to fulfil all righteousness." In the light of the holiness of His character, and the redemptive purpose of His mission, it is evident that to Him the baptism in water by John was the solemn act by which He assumed a responsibility which by nature He did not share. The multitudes whom John had baptized, had confessed their sins. Jesus had no sins of His own to confess, but by that act He

31

confessed their sins as His own ; and was numbered with transgressors, foreshadowing another baptism through which He would pass, in order to the accomplishment of His saving purpose. The King therefore is seen facing a kingdom in ruin, and consenting to the only method by which it could be redeemed. That was the meaning of His word " *Thus* it becometh us to fulfil all righteousness."

Matthew in four words tells the wonderful story, " Then he suffered Him," and one can only imagine the awe that must have filled the soul of John, himself a sinning man, as he was the instrument for giving expression to that tremendous assumption of responsibility for human sin on the part of the King.

ii. ANOINTING FOR OFFICE

The symbolic rite by which He had assumed responsibility being fulfilled, there was immediately granted to Him the specific equipment necessary for the fulfilment of His mission.

He was no stranger to the Spirit of God, even in the fact of His human nature. In the mystery of that nature He had been begotten by the Spirit, and throughout the years had lived the life truly Spirit-filled. But now as He moved to the high and holy vocation of His Messianic office, the heavens were opened above Him, and He saw the Spirit coming to Him in a form in which that Spirit had never been seen before, and in which He comes upon none other. The form of the dove was pre-eminently the symbol of sacrifice. In that Hebrew religious system created by Divine revelation, the dove was the sacrificial offering of the lowest and the humblest; and in a great unveiling of the necessity of holiness, and the compassion of God, the Holy Spirit in that form anointed the King for the fulfilment of that redeeming responsibility which He had now publicly assumed.

iii. ATTESTATION BY GOD

Immediately succeeding that specific

anointing a voice out of the heavens attested the Person and the purpose of the King. The attestation of the Person is found in the words, "This is My beloved Son," a great declaration casting its light back upon the story of the birth, and claiming the One Who stood unknown in the midst of the multitudes, as the definite and actual Son of God in every sense of the term. There He stood, identified with humanity in nature, and so closely in appearance that none distinguished a difference as between themselves and Him ; and yet separated from them in the very nature of His being, and in the actualities of His character.

The second part of the attestation consisted of the declaration of the Divine approval of His purpose, " in Whom I am well pleased." This word answers all questions with regard to the hidden years at Nazareth, and reveals the fact that in the ordinary life of the home, and the place of daily toil, He had realised the Divine ideal and satisfied the heart of His Father. And yet this word of approval

carries a profounder significance as it is
realised that it expressed the Divine appro-
bation of that action wherein He had
identified Himself with sinning men, in
order to fulfil all righteousness. As the
Spirit rested upon Him in sacrificial symbol,
so the voice of the Father declared the
Person of the King to be without blemish,
and His purpose to be in accord with the
determinate counsel and foreknowledge of
God.

III. HIS RELATION TO HELL

The opening word of this paragraph links it to that immediately preceding. " Then," after the opened heavens, hell was opened. The King must not only be in perfect harmony with the order and beauty and intention of the heavens. He must face all the disorder and ugliness and intention of the abyss. Goodness at its highest He knows, and is. Evil at its lowest He must face, and overcome. And so in the wilderness He is seen standing as humanity's representative between the two, responding to the one and refusing the other. The paragraph falls into three parts, the first stating the preliminary facts; the second giving an account of the testing; and the third recording the ultimate facts.

i. THE PRELIMINARY FACTS

The spiritual fact is first declared with great conciseness, but also with great clearness. The Person initiating the movement was the Spirit Who had descended upon

Him in the form of a dove, anointing the King for the specific work that lay before Him. The statement is at once arresting and remarkable that Jesus was "led up of the Spirit." The place is revealed in the statement that He " was led up . . . into the wilderness," and the form of the statement would suggest that He was taken from the valley of the Jordan where He had been baptized, to one of the desolate and barren mountain regions of the wilderness. He was thus cut off from other men, and from the means of sustenance. The most arresting value of this statement is that which declares the purpose. He was led there, not for the purpose of fellowship with God, nor for that of personal meditation, but " to be tempted of the devil."

The physical condition of the King in the hour of temptation is revealed as the second of the preliminary facts. His experience was that of fasting, and the time of His fasting was forty days, with the issue that He was conscious of hunger.

ii. THE TESTING

The first movement in the process of temptation was in the realm of the physical. The tempter suggested that if as the Divine voice had declared, He was the Son of God, He should exercise that power in order to provide for His material sustenance.

The assault was immediately repulsed as the King, recognising that He had been led into the wilderness by the Spirit of God, and that therefore the lack of sustenance was within the Divine purpose, declared His acceptation of the inspired teaching that the life of man could not be sustained by the sustenance of the physical, but by complete loyalty to the will of God, that is, by obedience to every word that proceeded out of ·the mouth of God.

The second movement in the process of temptation was in the realm of the spiritual. Being foiled in his attempt to overcome Jesus by appeal to His physical necessity, the enemy took Him to the holy city.

The method of the statement makes it impossible to think of this as merely an imaginative going to the temple. Dr. Vincent points out that the word "taketh" used of the action of the enemy, is exactly the same word used by each of the synoptists in describing the action of the Lord when He took the disciples to the mount of transfiguration. This entirely excludes the idea of many of the early writers that he carried Him through the air. It is evident that between the first and second temptation there was at least time for the journey to Jerusalem. Of course it must be remembered that at this time Jesus was not known to the crowds, and there is no reason to believe that Satan was visible to other eyes than those of the Lord Himself. There on the dizzy height, he suggested to Him again that if what God had said was true, that He was His Son, He should experiment in the realm of that relationship, and demonstrate His trust by the apparently heroic action of casting Himself down, in order to see whether the written word would be fulfilled in His experience, and no harm come to Him.

The assault was immediately repulsed as the Lord replied that " Thou shalt not tempt the Lord thy God " was the true law of trust, thus indicating that all such experiments would demonstrate doubt rather than confidence.

The third movement in the process of temptation was vocational. Again the enemy changed the scene as he conducted Him to " an exceeding high mountain," and there amid the suggestive splendour of the altitude, he made the kingdoms of the world and the glory of them pass in panoramic view before the vision of Jesus ; and offered to place Him in possession of them in return for homage rendered to himself.

The assault was again immediately repulsed as the Lord declared that the law which bound Him was that which declared that such homage and service must only be rendered to God.

Thus the King gloriously won in the

conflict. The attack was made against every vulnerable point; hunger, trust, and responsibility. When these are held, there remains no other avenue through which the foe can assault the citadel of the human will. The need of material sustenance, the confidence of the spirit in God, and the carrying out of a Divine commission in a Divine way; every gate was held by the King against the assault of the foe.

iii. The ultimate Facts

Full of suggestive beauty is the concluding declaration of the paragraph. Repulsed at every point the devil left Him, and immediately angels ministered unto Him. The departure of the devil was that of a vanquished enemy, the head and front of the offending under-world of evil, who had absolutely failed to find anything in the Man of God's right hand upon which he could fasten. We are not told the form or fashion of the angel ministry, but there can be no doubt that as at the commencement of the temptation the King was hungry, at the close He was conscious of physical weariness, and that angelic ministry would constitute a Divine seal upon the choices He had made in the process of temptation. He had refused to place Himself outside the Divine will by providing bread; and as in the case of the prophet of old, though for a very different reason, there can be little doubt that they fed Him with material bread. He had refused to make experiment upon His trust in God, in the hope that angels might protect Him from harm, and now they came, and their coming was the evidence of His Father's constant care. He had refused to take the kingdoms of the world by homage to Satan; and now those angels whom He will finally send out to administer the affairs of the Kingdom, came and served Him. Thus He is seen the victorious One over all the under-world of evil.

PARENTHESIS

This brief paragraph serves as an introduction to that which is immediately to follow. John alone gives us any account of that individual ministry in Jerusalem and Judæa, which followed immediately upon the baptism of Jesus in Jordan, John giving no account of the temptation. During that period however He had called to Himself Andrew, and in all probability John, Simon, Philip, and Nathanael; and was exercising this particular ministry while John the Baptist was still continuing to preach.

When the hour of John's arrest came, Jesus withdrew into Galilee, took up His abode in Capernaum, and from that time began His more definite and public propaganda.

44

B. HIS PROPAGANDA. iv. 17—xvi. 20

I. HIS ENUNCIATION OF LAWS. iv. 17—vii.

i. A NUCLEUS GATHERED. iv. 17—v. 2

a. THE COMMENCEMENT OF THE PROPAGANDA.
iv. 17
    1. *The Time.*
    2. *The Burden.*

b. THE CALLING OF HIS SUBJECTS. iv. 18-22
    1. *Simon and Andrew.* 18-20
    2. *James and John.* 21, 22

c. THE CAMPAIGN IN GALILEE. iv. 23-25
    1. *The Methods.* 23
      α. Teaching.
      β. Preaching.
      γ. Healing.

    2. *The Results.* 24, 25
      α. Report through Syria.
      β. Great healing Ministry.
      γ. Multitudes.

d. THE CRISIS OF REVELATION. v. 1, 2
    1. *The Occasion.* " *Seeing the Multitudes.*"
    2. *The Method.* " *His Disciples.*"
    3. *The Nature.* " *He taught them.*"

B. HIS PROPAGANDA

We now commence the central division of the Gospel which tells the story of the King's propaganda. He made Capernaum by the sea in the borders of Zebulun and Naphtali His base of operations, in all probability because it was a despised area, and held in contempt by Jerusalem and Judæa. That view is corroborated by the parenthesis immediately preceding this section, in which Matthew declared that His coming to Capernaum was in fulfilment of the prophecy of Isaiah, that light would spring up to those who dwelt in the region and shadow of death. The record of the propaganda falls into three sections, the first of which deals with His enunciation of laws ; the second with His exhibition of ability ; and the third with His enforcement of claims.

I. HIS ENUNCIATION OF LAWS

The section giving the account of the King's enunciation of laws first tells the

47

story of the gathering of a nucleus, and a preparatory ministry ; then records the great Manifesto ; and finally chronicles the immediate effect produced.

i. A Nucleus gathered

This section opens with a definite declaration of the commencement of the propaganda of the King as to its time and its burden. The time was that which had already been referred to ; the imprisonment of John and His own settlement in Capernaum. The burden of the propaganda in phrasing was exactly that of the herald, " Repent ye ; for the Kingdom of heaven is at hand." The implication is exactly the same, that men were in rebellion against God, and failing to realise the Kingdom of heaven on earth. The call was identical, that they should repent, reconsider the ideal, and re-adjust their lives to the Divine government. The declaration was the same, that the Kingdom of heaven was at hand. Immediately however, we shall see that the King went further than John.

48

John could only make the announcement and declare the imminence of Another. Christ was able to follow His own announcement with the definite words, " Follow Me," thus claiming for Himself the position of King.

Next in order we have the account of the calling of four of His subjects, and it must be carefully noticed that two of these, Simon and Andrew, had certainly already heard His call to discipleship. In all probability John also had heard the call, as it is more than probable that he was " the other " who accompanied Andrew, when under the influence of the preaching of John the Baptist, they followed the Christ. It may be that James now heard this call for the first time. In any case it is important that we notice that He now called these men, not to discipleship merely, but to fellowship with Himself in order to service. From this time they abandoned their daily avocation, and became His loyal subjects, associated with Him in His propaganda.

Having thus called these men into this closer fellowship, there followed a remark-

able campaign in Galilee, which Matthew
briefly but clearly described as to its methods
and results.

The first method referred to was that of
teaching in the synagogues, which was that
of the interpretation of their Scriptures.
The second was that of preaching good
tidings, which was almost certainly, so far
as men were able to receive it, an interpretation of His own mission ; a declaration
of the fact that He had come for the
establishment of that Kingdom for which
men had long waited, but which they had
been unable to realise. The third method
was that of healing all manner of disease and
all manner of sickness ; a ministry expressing
at once His compassion for human suffering,
and revealing His ability to deal with it.

The results of this campaign were most
remarkable. The report of Him went far
beyond Galilee, spreading as the record
declares " into all Syria," that is through
the whole Roman province bearing that
name, stretching to the north and east
of Galilee. The result of this was that

from all that region they brought to Him
" all that were sick, holden with divers
diseases and torments, possessed with devils,
and epileptic, and palsied," and He exercised
a great ministry of healing. The further
result was that great multitudes began to
follow Him wherever He went, and these
were gathered, not from the immediate
neighbourhood of Galilee only, but from
Decapolis and from Jerusalem and from
Judæa and from beyond Jordan. It is
quite evident that in these early stages of
His work, the material benefits of His
kingly rule attracted men, rather than the
spiritual principles He revealed.

It was these gathering multitudes which
created the crisis of revelation in His teaching, and called forth His systematic enunciation of laws. That crisis is carefully
described, in order to introduce the record
of the manifesto itself.

The occasion is indicated by the words,
" seeing the multitudes." These were made
up in the way described in the preceding
paragraph. It was a great mixed crowd of

people attracted, as we have said, by His power to cure disease, but in entire ignorance of the foundation principles of the Divine Kingdom. His vision of the multitudes caused Him to utter His manifesto. In a later section of our Gospel we shall find Matthew's account of how He saw the multitudes, and the effect the vision produced upon Him. He knew the Divine order, and as He looked upon these people, He saw how they were failing, and how they were suffering in consequence of failure; and in view of this His heart was moved with compassion for them.

The method He adopted for the enunciation of His laws is revealed in the declaration that He " went up into the mountain: and when He had sat down, His disciples came unto Him: and He opened His mouth and taught *them*." The sequel will show that multitudes gathered about the Lord and the inner circle of disciples, and heard the manifesto; but it is of the utmost importance that we recognise that He was speaking to the disciples.

There can be no question that His ultimate purpose was the establishing of the Kingdom of God among the crowds ; but He could only enunciate the laws of the Kingdom to souls who were loyal to the King ; and this is the explanation of His going of set purpose, to a mountain, and gathering about Him His own disciples.

The nature of the manifesto is revealed in the word " He *taught* them." Men everywhere were conscious of the need of the establishment of the Kingdom of God, and many were living in expectation of the coming of the King. But the ideal of the Kingdom held by such was a degraded ideal, being material and exclusive ; and in all likelihood this was true even of those who were following Him as disciples. It was necessary therefore that they should be taught the truth concerning these matters, and in order to this He uttered His manifesto, the fundamental revelations of which were that character is necessary in order to conduct, and right relation to the spiritual in order to the true realisation of the material.

ii. THE MANIFESTO

For purposes of systematic examination we may divide the manifesto into three parts, in the first of which the King laid down the fundamental principles of His Kingdom; in the second enunciated the laws thereof; and in the third uttered His words of final application.

a. THE FUNDAMENTAL PRINCIPLES

The statement of principles consists of a revelation of pattern; an indication of purpose; and a proclamation of principle.

1. *Revelation of Pattern. The Beatitudes*

In these opening declarations the King revealed the essential nature of His Kingdom, both as to His ultimate purpose, and as to the secret of realisation. The word *blessed*, with which each separate declaration commences, is in itself a revelation of purpose, as it marks the Divine will for man. A study of the conditions which are declared blessed will reveal the fact that in the

55

Kingdom of heaven the matter of supreme moment is character. The beatitudes fall into two groups, the first dealing with character ; and the second with conduct.

a. *The Seven. Of Character*

This sevenfold beatitude may be dealt with in many ways. The seven words indicate a growth, in which character proceeds from poverty of spirit to the activity which makes for peace.

They also constitute a unity, for any reward may be placed after any beatitude without violating the truth, thus showing that the King gave an analysis of character, rather than described different characteristics.

It is equally true that they suggest a sequence, for experimentally no man can enter into any of the conditions save upon the realisation of the one immediately preceding, the first of all being poverty of spirit.

Recognising that these words constitute an analysis of character, we shall briefly glance at each in order. Before doing so it is well that we should observe that the characteristics dealt with are those necessary in the present period of service and of conflict. In the ultimate establishment of the Kingdom of God, some of these qualities will find no place, because the occasion for them will have passed away. In that Kingdom there will be no mourning, no hunger and thirst after righteousness, no necessity for the exercise of mercy, or the activity which produces peace. Poverty of spirit, meekness of will, purity of heart will abide for ever.

Those who are " poor in spirit " are the true subjects of the King, and consequently they are His free men. Theirs is the Kingdom. They have the freedom of the city of God.

They that mourn are the true penitents, such as are conscious of their own past failure, which they consistently and increasingly deplore. Such are strong men, for they are comforted, and the word has all the values associated with the true

Kingdom, having entered by this very pathway of persecution.

He then uttered His word of blessing upon those in the midst of the process of suffering, bidding them rejoice and be exceeding glad, first because their reward in heaven would be great ; and secondly because in such suffering they were in fellowship with those who had gone before.

2. *Indication of Purpose*

Having thus revealed the pattern of the Kingdom in the character of its subjects, the King proceeded to indicate the immediate purpose. Such character will inevitably result in influence, and that is the Divine intention. The nature of this influence is revealed by the use of two figures.

The first is that of salt which is aseptic, that is, preventing the spread of corruption, and so preserving the possibility of goodness. It is necessary that all these figures should be carefully observed, and not carried

60

beyond the bound of their natural suggestion. Salt has no power to change the nature of that which is corrupt. The responsibility of the subjects of the Kingdom is that of maintaining the savour which constitutes the true value of salt ; and this can only be done as the character already described is realised.

The second figure is that of light, which is illuminative, and the King made a two-fold application of that figure. The first was that of a city set on a hill which cannot be hid, which suggests the illumination of broad expanses, the testimony of the fellowship of those within the Kingdom to the nature of that Kingdom. The second was that of the lamp in the house, suggesting the irradiation of all private places ; and emphasises the value of the individual testimony to the will of God in its effect upon the details of individual life. The responsibility connected with this aspect of influence is that of so shining before men that they may glorify the Father.

61

b. THE LAWS

The King now enunciated His moral code, and this falls into two parts, the first dealing with the laws of earthly relationships; and the second with those of heavenly relationships.

1. *Earthly Relationships*

In setting forth His laws of earthly relationships the King referred to certain words of the Mosaic economy, and thereby revealed the abiding force of all the great principles of human conduct contained in the law and the prophets. The righteousness which He came to make possible does not destroy the old, but fulfils it, that is, fills it to the full. The requirements of the new law will not be less exacting than the regulations of the old; they will go far beyond, and exceed them, dealing not merely with the details of externality, but with the attitudes and activities of the hidden life. These laws may be divided into three groups; those showing the foundations of society ; those indicating the pillars of society ; and that revealing the constitution of society.

a. *The Foundations of Society*

The first foundation of human society is the individual word which reveals the sacredness of life. The old law said " Thou shalt not kill." The King's interpretation of that law penalised, not merely the act of killing, but the attitudes of mind which make killing possible. Under the old economy the man who killed was declared to be in danger of the judgment ; and the word judgment in that connection must be interpreted by the law which declared that the penalty of murder was death. That same word was used by the King as describing the danger of the man who is angry with his brother. He further declared that he who uses the word Raca, a term of contempt, to his brother, is in danger of the discipline of the highest court ; and he who calls his brother a fool, a term of insult, is in danger of Gehenna. Thus no room

66

is left for murder. The provision of the Kingdom does not begin by arresting a criminal with blood-red hands. It arrests the man in whom the murder spirit is born. Finally the King indicated rules of procedure, observing which, His subjects would be delivered from the dangers indicated. No man must offer his gift on the altar of God, if his brother has aught against him, until he has sought reconciliation with him. There must be immediate agreement with the adversary, that is, the person wronged, who has just cause of complaint.

It is most interesting to note that while this ethic of Jesus forbids those attitudes of the mind which, unchecked, are likely to issue in murder; when He uttered these rules of procedure He had in mind, not the man likely to be angry because he was wronged, but the man whose wrong-doing had created the anger. This indeed is justice on the highest of all levels. No man must be angry with his brother, but his brother also must see to it that he gives him no cause for anger.

The second foundation of society is the social word which reveals the sacredness of marriage. The old law said "Thou shalt not commit adultery." The new interpretation penalises the desire which may issue in the act. These are the most searching words concerning impurity that were ever uttered, and in view of them the marriage relationship is lifted into a region full of awe. Here also the King gave rules observing which, all such unholy desire would be immediately corrected. His words are almost violent in their revelation of His thought on this matter. If the right eye cause a man to stumble, he is to pluck it out; or if the right hand offend, he is to cut it off. Of the perils of impurity of thought we do not often speak, and it is better so. Yet let the heart remember that the King has spoken, and no human words are necessary after the burning speech of the infinite Purity.

In this connection He quoted the word of the old economy which permitted a writing of divorcement ; and gave the new interpretation of that matter as He declared that the only reason for divorce is the sin of fornication.

β. *The Pillars of Society*

Human society according to the ethic of the King is to be supported upon the pillars of truth and justice.

With regard to truth He quoted the word from the old economy which safeguarded oaths. In His Kingdom, oaths are forbidden. The danger is recognised of taking the name of God in vain by using it in an oath, in support of falsehood. In the new Kingdom, character will make the oath unnecessary, and therefore simple affirmation or negation will be sufficient. This is ensured by the consciousness of God. When men remember that heaven is His throne, that earth is His footstool, that Jerusalem is His city, that the hairs of the head are white or black by His will ; in that consciousness of the connection of

69

everything with Him, their speech will be that of simple statement, and absolute truth.

With regard to justice the old law provided for retribution in kind, or what we now often speak of as poetic justice. "An eye for an eye, and a tooth for a tooth." That is always a righteous law for the governance of barbaric peoples. This the King actually changed as He commanded His subjects that they resist not evil, and that their action toward men is to be that of undeserved generosity. The old law reckoned with self, and attempted its conditioning. The new considers self as having lost its assertiveness in the will of the King. To the loyal soul whose greatest ambition is the coming of the Kingdom, there will always be a delight in accompanying the King on those excursions of undeserved generosity, which best reveal His heart. The other cheek, thy cloke also, the second mile, the constant gift, are the methods of revenge in the Kingdom ; and it is no wonder that men are astonished and

70

unbelieving until they have known the King.

γ. *The Constitution of Society*

The final word concerning earthly relationships is one which reveals the temper in which society will be cohesive and strong. The old law recognised division in its command, "Thou shalt love thy neighbour, and hate thine enemy." The new recognises relationship to God, and commands a temper which is the natural outcome thereof. The subjects of the King are to love as the sons of God. That love moreover, is not of that kind which "alters when it alteration finds." Its strength is to be in itself, rather than in the object. Enemies are to be loved, and the power for such loving is found in the fact of relationship to God. The final word of the King is at once tender and severe. " Ye therefore shall be perfect, as your heavenly Father is perfect." There must be no attempt to minimise the strictness of that great word. Let there rather be the determination to know and

71

obey the laws of the Kingdom, and so to realise its ideal by approximation to the character of God. It is only so, that love will be stronger than circumstances, triumph over wrong, and prove itself mightier than death.

2. *Heavenly Relationships*

In setting forth the laws of heavenly relationships the King referred to prevalent habits of life, rather than to laws of the old economy. He first laid down a general principle ; and then made applications of it in the spiritual and material realms.

a. *The general Principle*

In this statement the revisers substituted the word righteousness for alms, a reading which is approved of almost unanimously by the great editors and scholars. The change harmonises too with the general movement. As immediately before the actual enunciation of laws the King had laid down a principle, that the righteousness of His subjects must exceed that of scribes and Pharisees, He now in the midst of that enunciation reveals the difference between the righteousness to which He calls men, and that of the scribes and Pharisees. Moreover He deals with the subject of alms immediately afterwards, that being only a part of a greater whole, with which the King was about to deal, in the matter of the laws of spiritual life.

This enunciation of a general principle takes the form of a warning, in the implication of which we find the positive principle to be remembered. It is a statement of a new motive for conduct, and is a most searching word, going to the inner source of all action. A thought, a reason, a purpose precedes all deeds, and this word of the King probes the region of that reason. The warning is against the cultivation of a righteousness in order that it may be seen of men ; and the implication is that the motive for righteousness is that of being well pleasing to the Father. To do righteousness to be seen of men robs it of its value, and those who do so have no reward of God. To do righteousness for its own sake, and because it is in harmony with the will of God is the only way which makes righteousness of any value. To be honest because honesty is the best policy, is to have no credit for honesty in the ledgers of heaven. To do right only because men are looking, is to be unrewarded of God ; for the probability is that if men were not looking, the exact opposite might be done. It is with that choice of the heart that the ethic of the Kingdom deals.

β. *Spiritual Applications*

This principle is now applied in the activities of the spiritual life, of which there are three ; alms, prayer, and fasting.

Outward.   Alms

The giving of alms is an outward, spiritual activity.   On the level of strict justice and equity there is no need for any such action. When men give alms it is in response to some spiritual impulse which may be either bad or good.   The false method is described as that of the giving of alms with ostentatious publicity, in order that the one bestowing the gifts, may have glory of men.   Of such giving the King declared that the men indulging therein have received their reward. If a man gives alms to be seen of men, and is seen of men, he gains what he desires, but there is no value in the action beyond.

The law of the King is that the giving of alms is to be in secret; and the King declared that such giving is seen of the Father, and is recompensed by Him. A subject of the King, no longer desirous of the applause of his fellow men, quietly and secretly helps the needy, and the deed is recognised by God, and by Him is recompensed. Sir Moses Montifiore, a devout Hebrew, held it as a sacred principle of giving, that announced and acknowledged generosity had its only reward therein, and did not count in the reckoning of Jehovah; and that is exactly what the King taught in this manifesto.

Heavenward. *Prayer*

In the next paragraph we find the application of the same principle to the exercise of prayer. Again the false method is indicated, that of the hypocrites, who love to stand and pray in order to be seen of men. It is

not wrong to pray at the street corners.   It
is wrong to pray there to be seen of men ;
and again, of those who pray in this way,
the King said "they have received their
reward."

To His subjects He then revealed the
true method of prayer ; first as to its place.
The true place of prayer is the inner
chamber with the door closed.   There
prayer is to be offered to the Father Who
is in secret, and Who seeth in secret, and
He will recompense.   Moreover in the
practice of true prayer there is to be no
need for vain repetitions.   God has not to
be persuaded into giving by our much
speaking.   Before we ask Him He knows
the things we have need of.   Our asking
therefore may be in all confidence, and in
all simple directness.

It was at this time that the King gave to
His subjects the great pattern prayer, every
sentence of which is full of meaning, and
the comprehensiveness of which leaves
nothing outside its scope.   It may be
broadly divided into two parts.   In the first

of these the subject prays for the rights of the King, and in the second for the needs of the subjects of the Kingdom. It is of great importance that in the study of this prayer we should observe the fact that our Lord emphasised one of its petitions by a word of exposition and exhortation; for it is singular that this particular petition is the one which has been most often modified in the form in which the prayer has been used. It is that which asks " Forgive us our debts, as we also have forgiven our debtors." Concerning that, the King declared that if His subjects forgive men their trespasses, their Father will forthem; and with equal clearness that if they do not forgive men, their Father will not forgive them. Of course it must be recognised that these words are words spoken to those within the Kingdom.

Inward. Fasting

Again the false method is indicated which is that of drawing attention to the fact of fasting by the sadness of countenance, and

80

the disfigurement of the face. Once again the word of the King is heard concerning those who follow this method. " They have received their reward."

The true reason of fasting is to be found in the opportunity it affords for a clearer vision of God, and that must ever manifest itself in new gladness of face. Sadness of face reveals the fact that the person fasting is more occupied with the act than with the ultimate intention. That fasting which consists of the giving up of anything perfectly legitimate in itself, in order that we may increase our power in communion with God, will ever issue in the increase of joy and its manifestation, as, facing life, we reveal the peace and the delight of knowing God.

γ. *Material Applications*

The King proceeded to the enunciation of those laws which apply the heavenly relationships to material matters.

Concerning wealth His subjects are to be without covetousness. The false attitude toward wealth is that which lays it up selfishly, and moreover foolishly, upon the earth where it is liable to depreciation and destruction.

He then revealed the true attitude toward earthly wealth. He did not say that it was wrong to possess earthly treasure. He did say that it was wrong to lay it up for self. It is to be held as by stewards. At best, earthly treasure is valueless, by comparison with true riches. His estimate of it is seen in the words "moth and rust consume," "thieves break through and steal." What gentle irony is found in these descriptions, and what quiet contempt they reveal for the things which men hold dear. These things harbour their own instruments of destruction, moth and rust; and allure the thieves, who take with them the moth and rust also, so that their gain of iniquity is doomed. All this is poor, and hardly worth the labour of laying up at all. The true treasure is that which is laid up beyond the reach of moth and rust and thief. How treasure is to be laid up in that safe place the King revealed, as dealing with the whole man He declared that where the treasure is the heart is, that if the eye be single, the whole body is full of light. No man can serve two masters. If the emotional life be centred in spiritual and heavenly things, then treasure will be laid up in that realm. If the intellectual life be unified as the eye is single, seeing only the glory of God, all wealth will be consecrated to Him. If the volitional life be under the dominion of God rather than mammon, then men will use the mammon of un-righteousness in the interest of the Kingdom of God.

A further material application of heavenly relationships was that concerning the neces-sities of life; and here the subjects of the Kingdom are to be without care. The false method is that of anxiety for personal life, as to the things which are wholly material. The falsity of this method the King exposed by His question, " Is not the life more than the food, and the body than the raiment ? "

He then proceeded to reveal the true attitude of the subjects of the Kingdom toward all these necessary things of life. He did this first by illustrations. He declared that the birds of the heaven which neither sow nor reap nor gather, are fed by the Father; and inquired, " Are not ye of much more value than they ? " In the question two truths are involved, first that if God care for the birds He will certainly care for His children; but secondly that the children are endowed with higher capacities than the birds, which fact is in itself an argument for the greater care of God. The birds do not know how to sow, or reap, or gather, but His children do; and this capacity is part of His Divine beneficence. Why then should they be anxious ? So also as to raiment. The lilies of the field grow, though they cannot toil, nor are they able to spin; and their raiment is more glorious even than that of Solomon. And again, by the question He asked, the Lord made the same appeal to His subjects to abandon anxiety.

84

Finally He turned from illustration to definite instruction as He charged them first, that they should not be anxious about material things, because their Father knew their need; secondly, that they should seek His Kingdom, resting assured that all the things they needed would be added to them; and finally, that they should not be anxious for the morrow, because the evil of a day is enough for a man to face within the compass of the day.

c. THE FINAL APPLICATIONS

Having thus enunciated the actual laws of His Kingdom, the King uttered His words of final application. These deal with the dynamic which creates the possibility of obedience ; the threefold responsibility which confronts the subjects of the King ; and the last and supreme claim which He made concerning His teaching.

1. *The Dynamic*

The central teaching of this paragraph concerns the provision which is made in the Divine economy for the direct dealing of man with God. In preparation for that, the attitude of the subjects of the King toward others is carefully described ; and finally their activity toward others is defined.

a. The Attitude

Their attitude is to be characterised by the absence of censoriousness. No man is to constitute himself the judge of his brother. Against such judgment the King definitely warned His subjects. The first argument in enforcement of the warning consists of the statement of the principle that human judgment will be responded to by human judgment in kind. Moreover the difficulty in the way of forming a correct judgment is that of the imperfection of every man. While he may pass judgment on the mote in the eye of his brother, his ability to see that clearly, is hindered by the beam in his own eye. If it be necessary that the mote be removed from the eye of a man, the one attempting to remove it must first see to it that the beam is removed from his own eye.

The attitude of the subjects of the Kingdom toward those who are essentially and persistently evil must be that of caution. It is necessary that there should be discrimination in dealing with holy and precious things, for dogs and swine have no understanding of their value. Within the Kingdom all judgment rests with the King, but there must be a clear understanding of the line of separation that exists between loyalty and rebellion ; and while brethren may not judge brethren, all the subjects of the King are to pass this judgment on such as are notoriously persistent in evil courses, that they are incapable of receiving the things which pertain to the Kingdom, and therefore the holy and precious things must not be offered to them.

β. *The Provision*

Perhaps in the whole course of the manifesto nothing is more calculated to reveal the altitude of the ideal of the King, or the impossibility of obedience thereto, so clearly as this description of attitude which we have considered. It is therefore an arresting fact that at this point, as the bewildered soul is almost in despair, the King uttered the glorious words which reveal the secret of power available, in order to fulfilment. The declaration consists of a command and a statement. The command is threefold, and consists of the repetition of the same idea in different words, all intended to emphasise and simplify the teaching ; ask, seek, knock ; and side by side with each form of command there is a definite promise, " it shall be given . . . ye shall find . . . it shall be opened." The statement is absolute and unequivocal that " every one that asketh receiveth ; and he that seeketh findeth ; and to him that knocketh it shall be opened."

Then in great grace, and in order to help those who heard Him to place their confidence in His declaration, the King appealed to them by the argument of their own natural affection, as He suggested by His questions that in the case of any one of them, if a son should ask for a loaf he would not give him a stone, or for a fish he would not give him a serpent. Applying the illustration, He emphasised it by indicating the infinite distance between themselves and their Father in heaven, as He reminded them that they were evil, and yet would know how to give good gifts to their children ; and again in the form of a question declared that the Father in heaven,

90

Himself essentially good, would certainly give good things to them that ask Him.

γ. *The Activity*

In view of that provision made for the supply of human need by God, in answer to human application, the King summarised the whole of His ethical teaching so far as man's relationship to man is concerned, in what to-day we describe as the golden rule. In our study of that great saying of the Lord we must never forget to lay emphasis upon the word " therefore." Because we may ask, and have; seek, and find; knock, and know the door opened ; our activity toward our fellow men is to be that of the righteousness which is the outcome of love.

2. *The threefold Responsibility*

Having thus revealed the dynamic in the power of which men may fulfil the ethic, the King proceeded to reveal a threefold responsibility, that namely of entrance upon the way, of guidance in obedience, and of the realisation of the issue ; or inclusively, responsibility concerning the way, the truth, and the life.

a. *The Way*

The King first indicated the necessity for entering by the narrow gate. He thus passed back to the first things He had said, and reminded those who listened to Him that the gracious beatitudes which He had uttered at the commencement, were nevertheless revelations of a severe requirement. In order to the appropriation of the benefits of the Kingdom there must be conformity to the standard of character. Moreover by this word He reminded them again of the sternest things He had said concerning the necessity for the mutilation of the physical life, if necessary, in the interest of the purity of the soul. All the severity of His requirement as revealed in the course of His teaching, is for ever calculated to halt such as are crowding after Him. In order to urge them to follow at all costs, He called men to enter by the strait gate, and graciously revealed the reason of its narrowness as He declared that the gate is wide and the way broad which leads to destruction ; while the gate is narrow and the way straitened that leads to life. The true value of this statement is only discovered as we observe that the broad way narrows to destruction ; while the straitened way broadens into fulness of life. Human responsibility is that of consenting to the stripping and denial which are necessary in order to entrance upon that way.

β. *The Truth*

Having entered upon the way, a new responsibility is created, which concerns the truth. The prophet is the interpreter of the will of God, and the King knew that a peril would confront those who yielded to Him, through false prophets, who would present themselves in the garb of truth, but whose nature would be that of ravening wolves. The responsibility of His subjects is that of not being deceived. Therefore He gave them the test by which all

93

prophets may be known.   It is that of fruit. He twice repeated the declaration, " By their fruits ye shall know them," and emphasised the statement by declaring the test to be inevitable, that a good tree must bring forth good fruit, and a corrupt tree must bring forth evil fruit, this being an inevitable law. The test is not an immediate one. There must be time ; and consequently the true attitude of the subjects of the King must be that of a careful reserve of judgment in the case of any interpretation which has not been vindicated by the fruitfulness of those advancing it.

γ. *The Life*

As the first word of responsibility had to do with the beginning, and the second with the progressive experience, the last is a responsibility created in view of the final issues. The life within the Kingdom is not that of profession merely. Calling the King Lord is not enough. There must be the actual doing of the will of the

Father. This teaching is rendered emphatic by the illustration the King used as He referred to the day of the final establishment of the Kingdom of Heaven ; and warned men that, not because they prophesied by His name, or by His name had cast out demons, or by His name done mighty works, would they find entrance. If in spite of these things they were disobedient to the teaching, and rebellious against the will of God, they would be rejected. A profession of loyalty which is not sincere, is profanation, and service rendered which is not purely motived, is sacrilege.

3. *The final Words*

The last words of the manifesto are supreme in the claim which the King made for His own teaching. This claim was made pictorially as He used the figure of the builders' craft, with which He was familiar in the experience of His human life in Nazareth ; and described the difference between permanent and perishing building.

a. *Permanent Building*

The condition of building character so that it may abide is that of hearing and doing His sayings. The test of such building will come in the day of stress and storm, when the rain descends, and the floods come, and the winds blow and beat upon the house. When a house is built upon a rock, no storms can destroy it. When a life is fashioned according to His teaching in this manifesto, no destructive force is equal to its undoing, for it is founded upon a rock, and stands.

β. *Perishing Building*

The condition of building character which will not abide is that of hearing His sayings, and not doing them. It is important that we should observe that there is no application of this word of Jesus to those who have never heard His words, or known His Gospel. It can only be applied in the case of those who are familiar with His teaching. Here again the test is the same.

It is that of the sweeping hurricane. When a house is built upon the sand, it crumbles before the force of the tempest. When a life is fashioned in disobedience to His ideals, it is an easy prey to the forces which destroy, for it is built upon the sand, and falls.

iii. THE EFFECT PRODUCED

It is evident as we suggested at the beginning, that while the words of the manifesto were addressed primarily to the group of disciples, the multitudes had followed the King and His subjects to the mountain height, and had listened to His teaching, for Matthew has recorded the effect produced, and the reason thereof. The effect was that of a great astonishment, and the reason of the astonishment was the authority of His teaching.

At first it might seem as though something in the manner of Jesus had impressed the crowds with His authority. Now while admitting that there must inevitably have been a dignity and authority in the very way in which He spoke; there can be no doubt that this very manner was created by the things which He said. This is borne out by the statement that " He taught as having authority, and not as their scribes," which statement is the more remarkable when we remember that the scribes were the authoritative teachers. Consequently the astonishment was created by a contrast of authorities. The authority of the scribe was that of official and dogmatic interpretation. The authority of the King was that of the self-evident truth of His teaching; and an unbiassed study of the manifesto to-day must produce the same effect. The only criticism which is at all warranted on the part of man is that the ideal is too high for his obedience. As to the splendour of that ideal there can be no question.

Thus in the process of His propaganda the King had now formally enunciated His laws, and therein revealed the order of the Kingdom of heaven which He had come to establish upon the earth.

II. HIS EXHIBITION OF ABILITY

The next stage in the propaganda of the King was that of the resumption of the activity of His power, following upon the enunciation of His ethic. The multitudes had listened to the wondrous words which He had spoken to His disciples, and had been astonished at the authority of His teaching. It was necessary now that in the light of that teaching His power should be further revealed. He had already exercised a great ministry of healing. In the comparatively brief section now devoted to the account of His exhibition of ability, we have three distinct movements.

i. FIRST MOVEMENT

In this movement we have the account of four manifestations of power, and of the results following thereupon.

a. THE MANIFESTATIONS

In this section the power of the King was manifested in dealing with leprosy, palsy, fever, and demons and disease.

1. *Leprosy. A Leper*

It is an arresting fact that immediately following upon the enunciation of His ethic, the King was met in the valley by a leper. In imagination one can see the multitudes accompanying Him, shrinking back to make way for the leper, in order that they might fulfil the requirement of the ancient law, and escape contamination. Apparently unheeding the crowd, the leper came into the presence of the King in the attitude of reverence, and in the words he addressed to Him, expressed confidence in His power ; and uncertainty as to His willingness.

The answer of the King was immediate, and to the multitudes surrounding it must have been startling. He stretched forth His hand and touched him, and affirming His willingness, demonstrated His ability to deal with leprosy. Our familiarity with the power of the Lord may interfere with our ability to realise how striking a demonstration of power this was to the people who witnessed it. In the economy of Moses there was no hope for the leper, and the moral requirements of that economy were most strict as to the absolute necessity for the segregation of leprosy, so that men not affected thereby, should not in any way come into contact with it. Yet here was the One Whose moral code had demanded a spiritual purity which seemed wellnigh impossible of achievement, touching the leprous man, and communicating to him a purity that cleansed him.

2. *Palsy. A Roman*

The next manifestation of power is equally impressive as to those in whose interest it was made. In this case a Roman soldier approached the King on behalf of his personal servant. It was the coming of one outside the covenant of Hebraism on behalf of another outside that covenant. The manner of his coming was that of a remarkable recognition of the method of the King's authority. Illustrating from his own position, that of a man being under authority, and therefore exercising authority over others, he besought the Lord to speak the word, and affirmed his conviction that if He would do so, his servant would be healed. It was the approach of one confident of the King's authority.

The King had interrupted the centurion's application in that before he had asked for a benefit, and had only told the story of the boy, He had said, " I will come and heal him." When the centurion had confessed his own unworthiness, and his confidence in the power of the King to act without taking the journey, Jesus made his confession the occasion of a solemn word of warning to the multitudes that were about Him. He was about to confer a benefit on a man outside the covenant, and He declared that was a type of what would happen in larger degree. He then uttered the word of power, and the servant was healed.

3. *Fever. A Woman*

The third manifestation of power was exercised on behalf of a woman, and this

time unasked. Entering into the house of
Peter, He saw a woman lying sick of a
fever, and immediately touched her hand,
and she was healed.

The demonstration of the completeness
of the healing was immediate as she arose
and expressed her gratitude in service
rendered to Him.

4. *Demons and Disease. Mixed Multitudes*

The last manifestation of power in this
first group of incidents took place on an
eventful evening. The story is very briefly
told, but suggests a picture full of beauty.
The King is seen surrounded by multitudes
who are bringing to Him those possessed
with demons, and those who were sick;
and His power is revealed in that without
any apparent difficulty, but merely by the
uttering of His word, He cast out the
demons and healed all that were sick. In
this connection however, Matthew reveals
the secret of that wonderful activity which
at the time he certainly did not know.
All that which appeared to be the activity

of absolute and abounding power was the
outcome of a profounder activity of suffering and of sacrifice, which had been foretold
by the prophet Isaiah in the great declaration, " Himself took our infirmities, and
bare our diseases."

In these things there had been a marvellous
revelation of His power ; leprosy, palsy, fever,
demons and disease ; all had obeyed His
touch or His word ; and His activity had
been marked by a gracious disregard of
human limitations as He had bestowed
benefits upon a leper, a Roman, a woman ;
all the despised of the Hebrew mind. By
these gifts He expressed His willingness to
include those on whom they were bestowed,
in His Kingdom. On that wonderful evening, when the crowds gathered, and the King
in a mystery which no human mind could
understand, took their infirmities and bare
their diseases, He gave a radiant revelation
not only of His power, but also of His love.

b. THE RESULTS

The first result of this activity of the

King was that of the gathering to Him of yet greater multitudes, and in view of this He gave commandment to depart unto the other side. While the multitudes were attracted principally by the benefits He conferred, there were those amongst them who were conscious of a desire to follow Him, and two illustrations are given.

The first is that of a scribe who in response to a splendid impulse said to Him, " I will follow Thee whithersoever Thou goest." To such an outcry the King made instantaneous reply, not intended to discourage, but to reveal that such following must inevitably mean fellowship in the experience of want and of homelessness. The illustration is left at that point. We have no right to say that this man did not follow.

The second illustration is that of a disciple who, moved by a similar desire, was yet divided between immediate loyalty to the King and his duty to his father; for it must be remembered that the phrase "suffer me first to go and bury my father" does not suggest that His father was dead, but that he desired to remain with him until he should die. To that suggestion the King replied, " Follow Me ; and leave the dead to bury their own dead," thus showing that no merely human tie must be allowed to interfere between His subjects and Himself.

ii. SECOND MOVEMENT

In this second movement we have again the account of four manifestations of power, and of the results following.

a. THE MANIFESTATIONS

The exhibition of the King's ability was now given in the material, the mental, and the moral realms; as He stilled the storm, healed the demoniacs, forgave sins, and captured the will.

1. *The Storm. The Disciples*

A manifestation of power over the elements was granted to His disciples only. Acting under His direction they had followed Him into a boat in order to cross to the other side. In the course of their crossing a great tempest arose, and the few words of Matthew present a striking picture. The boat was imperilled by waves which covered it, but in the midst of the storm the King was asleep. In their despair they awoke Him. His response was strange and

MATT. 113 I

Kingly. It consisted of a twofold rebuke, first of them for lack of faith, and then of the sea, producing the very calm they desired. That revelation of power filled the disciples with wonder, and drove them to the consciousness that they had not yet perfectly understood their Master. This is revealed in their question, " What manner of man is this, that even the winds and the sea obey Him ? "

2. *The Demoniacs. The City*

The arrival on the other shore was signalised by the approach of two demoniacs of so fierce a nature as to be a constant menace to the peace and safety of the country-side. If the disciples were uncertain as to Who the Lord was, these evil spirits had no such uncertainty. They recognised, and immediately confessed Him as the Son of God. They also were conscious of His purpose in the world, and expected that they would be cast out, for they requested that if this were done, they might be permitted to enter into a herd of swine.

114

In this request there is further demonstration of their understanding of the mission
of the King. They knew Him as Hebrew
Messiah, and understood that the traffic in
swine was forbidden to the people among
whom at that time He was exercising His
ministry.

To their request He immediately replied
in the word of authority, which sent them
forth from the man, and so delivered him
from his affliction, and the neighbourhood
from his evil influence, while at the same
time it destroyed the forbidden traffic.

The account of the wonder wrought
speedily reached the city, with the result
that their commercial catastrophe made
them insensible of the benefit which had
been conferred upon them by the healing
of the man, and they came out and besought Jesus that He would depart from
their borders.

This manifestation of the King's power
was accompanied by a revelation of the
limitation of His power. If the city will
not have Him, He will not force His

entrance ; and turning round, He re-entered
the boat, and crossed back to the other
side.

3. *The Forgiveness of Sins. A Man*

The King now exercised His authority in
a new way. There was brought to Him a
man sick of the palsy, and He immediately
answered the faith of those who brought
him, but not in the way which they expected. He pronounced pardon upon a
sinner, and straightway opposition was
aroused. Certain of the scribes who were
present thought within themselves that it
was a word of blasphemy, for they rightly
believed that none could forgive sins other
than God. In answer to their thought the
King suggested a problem as to whether it
was easier to forgive sins, or to heal disease.
As they heard His question, it suggested a
contrast. As a matter of fact it indicated a
connection, and in order that they might
know that He had authority to forgive sins,
He immediately healed the man sick of the
palsy. If they heard the question as sug-

gesting two exercises of power, then it was for them to decide which was easier, for He had claimed both, and one claim was vindicated by the actuality of the healed man. Or if they now were able to see the connection between the two, they would understand His teaching that all His healing miracles were based upon His ability to deal with the sin which lay at the root of human suffering. Whatever effect was produced upon the men who were in difficulty, the multitudes were filled with fear, and glorified God Who had given such power to men.

4. *The Will. Matthew*

There immediately followed a further illustration of His power, that of His constraint of the human will. As He moved away, unacknowledged as King by the vast masses of men, and therefore misunderstood and criticised, He saw Matthew, a publican, despised of his countrymen by reason of his calling; and looking on him, He said, " Follow Me."

117

The response was immediate and remarkable. He arose and followed Him, and although here in his Gospel he does not himself chronicle the fact, it was he who spread the feast in his own house at which Jesus sat down with publicans and sinners, as well as His own disciples.

b. THE RESULTS

In some senses the results of these manifestations of power are to be found in the course of the stories themselves. The disciples wondered and were compelled to inquire as to who and what manner of Man He was. The Gadarenes were made so conscious of the effect which His presence would produce in the interests of righteousness that they were constrained to send Him away. The multitudes glorified God as they saw the man sick of the palsy healed ; and the despised publican found the King, and yielding to Him was prepared for the high office of writing the Gospel which should reveal Him as King.

Here however, two illustrations are given

of the results which His methods produced. The first is that of the Pharisees who were perplexed by His willingness to sit down and eat with publicans and sinners. He answered their perplexity by explaining His own action, and declaring that His mission was that of healing, in all the full sense of the word; affirming that He had not come to call the righteous, but sinners.

The second illustration is that of the disciples of John who were perplexed by the joy of the disciples of Jesus. Their own religious outlook, in common with that of the Pharisees, necessitated the practice of fasting; but the disciples of Jesus did not fast. In reply to this inquiry He declared the reason to be that of His own presence amongst them, declaring that the days would come when they would fast; and further He affirmed the reasonableness of the methods which these men could not understand, by the figure of the wine and the wine-skins; which taught the truth that the new campaign necessitated new modes of expression.

iii. THIRD MOVEMENT

Once again we have four manifestations of power, followed by a brief declaration of the results following.

a. THE MANIFESTATIONS

In this paragraph we see the power of the King over death, disease, darkness, and demons.

1. *Death. The Child of Jairus*

While the King was yet replying to the inquiry of the disciples of John, a ruler approached Him with a story of over-whelming sorrow. He came in reverence, and in faith, declaring that all hope of help through ordinary methods had gone as he said, " My daughter is even now dead"; but affirming his conviction that the touch of Jesus would restore her.

The answer of the King was immediate. He arose and followed Jairus. On the way, in the healing of the woman, He gave Jairus an illustration of His power, which must have confirmed his faith and strengthened his hope. Arriving at the house of Jairus, with dignity and authority He sent the tumultuous mourning crowd about their business, and then did exactly what Jairus had suggested. He laid His hand upon the child, and immediately she responded to the touch. This was the first time in which the King had manifested His power in the awful realm of death. It is not to be wondered at that the fame of Him went forth into all the land.

2. *Disease. A Woman*

On the way to the house of Jairus, in the illustration of power to which we have referred, there was one of the most beautiful of all the revelations of that power. The King was surrounded by His disciples, and the multitude that followed. It must have been difficult for any one to get very near to Him. The woman had been for twelve years the victim of a form of disease which subjected her to every kind of disadvantage and disability. She was excommunicated from the assemblies in the synagogue, divorced from her husband, and ostracised from society. Nevertheless she found her way to the King, and touched the border of His garment. It was an activity inspired by faith as her thought, afterwards declared, undoubtedly reveals, " If I do but touch His garment, I shall be made whole."

The answer of the King is full of beauty. It was a word of comfort, and a deed of power. He understood all that she had suffered, and turning round and looking into her eyes, He called her Daughter, and bade her be of good cheer. From that hour she was made whole.

3. Darkness. *Two blind Men*

After the raising of Jairus' child, and as the King passed on His way, He was followed by two blind men who cried out, "Have mercy on us, Thou Son of David." The form of address was remarkable. It was really a recognition of Messiahship. It may not have been wholly intelligent. Probably it was an expression of hope, and of venture based upon it, as the result of what they had heard of His power in the case of the child raised from the dead. He does not seem to have made any immediate reply, for it was not until He had entered the house, and the men had followed Him, that He spoke to them. He then challenged their faith, asking them if they believed that He was able to do what they asked. They immediately replied "Yea, Lord," thus affirming their faith, and addressing Him in the language of reverent respect. The King immediately responded to their faith, and their eyes were opened.

Here we have one of the occasions when the Lord strictly charged them not to tell the story of how they had received their sight. They, in all probability with the best intention, disobeyed His command, and going forth, spread abroad His fame.

4. *Demons. A dumb Man*

The last manifestation of power recorded in this group is that of the casting out of a demon, and the loosing of a dumb tongue. It is interesting to note that Matthew gives no details. The power of the King was being exercised so perpetually that he simply declares that a man was brought to Him in this condition, and proceeds to the story of results produced by saying, "When the demon was cast out, the dumb man spake: and——."

b. THE RESULTS

This last manifestation of power culminating a series, produced a twofold result. The multitudes marvelled and affirmed their conviction that such wonders had never been seen in Israel. In this connection the opposition of His foes manifested itself more definitely, and the long conflict with the forces of false religion began. The Pharisees, madly jealous of His power, attributed it to Satan. One wonders more and more at the grace which bore so patiently with these men. It does not seem that at the time the King vouchsafed any answer to their awful suggestion; and yet how it must have pained His sacred heart, this wilful misinterpretation of His deeds of grace. The evil of it lay in the fact that it was intended to divert the crowds from their wonder and admiration, and stir up their fear and animosity; and this action was taken by the men who should have been the shepherds of the people. It is well that we remember this, as it has its bearing on the section immediately to follow.

III. HIS ENFORCEMENT OF CLAIMS. ix. 35—xvi. 20

i. HIS HELPERS. ix. 35—x.

a. THE CAUSE. ix. 35, 36

1. *The King's Mission.* 35
   All the Cities and Villages.
   Teaching. Preaching. Healing.

2. *The King's Vision.* 36a
   The Multitudes. Distressed.
   Scattered.
   Not having a Shepherd.

3. *The King's Compassion.* 36b

b. THE COMMISSION. ix. 37—x. 5a

1. *The Vision of Harvest.*
2. *The Call to Prayer.* 37
3. *The Equipment for Service.* 38
4. *The Names of the Twelve.* x. 1
5. *The Appointment.* 2-4
   5a

c. THE CHARGE. x. 5b-42

1. *The First Work.   Until the Cross.* x. 5b-15
   a. *The limited Sphere.* 5b, 6
   β. *The Nature of the Work.* 7, 8
   γ. *The Method of the Work.* 9-15
   No Provision for Need.
   Hospitality of the Worthy.
   An Alternative of Peace or Judgment.

2. *The second Period of Service. " Till the*
   Son of Man be come." x. 16-23
   α. *The Time of Peril.* 16a
   β. *The necessary Qualifications.* 16b
   γ. *Warnings and Instructions.* 17-23
   Beware of Men.
   Be not anxious. . . . The Spirit.
   The Time of Division.
   From City to City.

3. *The third Period. To the End of the*
   Age. x. 24-42
   a. *Identification in Misunderstanding.* 24, 25
   β. *Identification in Testimony.* 26-33
   The Proclamation of His Word. 26, 27
   The Protection of the Father. 28-31
   The Reward of Confession. 32, 33
   γ. *Identification in Suffering.* 34-39
   The coming Divisions. 34-36
   The Re-ponsibility of Fellowship. 37-39
   δ. *Identification in Victory.* 40-42
   Their Reception, His Reception. 40
   Ministry to them, Ministry to Him. 41, 42

III. HIS ENFORCEMENT OF CLAIMS

We now come to the final section of the division of the Gospel dealing with the propaganda of the King. It is chiefly characterised by the hostility manifested toward Him, and consequently by His enforcement of claims. There are four movements in the section, dealing respectively with His helpers, His difficulties, His conflict, and His victory.

i. His Helpers

We have now reached a crisis at which the King called His chosen twelve into association with Himself in actual service; and in this first movement we have the account of that appointment, as to its cause, His commissioning of the twelve, and the charge He delivered to them.

a. THE CAUSE

Matthew now referred to the general mission of the King through all the cities and villages. It had been a ministry of teaching, preaching, and healing.

His reference to this was in order to a declaration concerning the King's vision of the people. The description of that is pre-eminently in the terms of Kingship according to Biblical interpretation. It was Homer who said "All kings are shepherds of the people," and it is certainly true that the Divine conception of Kingship as revealed in the Bible is ever that of the shepherd. It was thus that the King looked upon the multitudes, and He saw them distressed and scattered. The words are full of suggestiveness, and reveal the people as sheep, harried by wolves, fleeced, wounded, fainting by the way; and to the eyes of the King they were in this condition because they had no shepherd.

The central declaration of the paragraph is that in consequence of His vision, the King was moved with compassion. That compassion was the reason of His action in commissioning the twelve, and sending them forth.

b. THE COMMISSION

In calling these men to new service, He first gave them a vision of the conditions from the standpoint of His need of their aid as He said, " The harvest truly is plenteous, but the labourers are few." The people who appeared to Him as distressed and scattered from the standpoint of their need, appeared as a harvest, waiting to be gathered, in view of His ability, and of His need of helpers. Having made this declaration to the disciples He called them to prayer, not for the people, but that the Lord of the harvest should send forth labourers. Having thus instructed them to pray, He called the twelve to Him in a new sense, and equipped them for the work they were immediately to do, by giving them authority over demons, and to heal disease and sickness. The names of the twelve are chronicled with certain suggestive descriptions in the case of some of them, and the fact of their appointment is recorded.

c. THE CHARGE

Before their departure, the King gave them a solemn charge in view of their work. A careful study of this will make it evident that while He was referring to work which lay immediately before these men, His mind travelled on to work which they would have to do at a later period; and even beyond, to the work of all His disciples to the end of the age which His commission initiated. The charge therefore had to do with three periods of work; the first work until the Cross; the second period of service till the Son of man be come; and the third period to the end of the age.

1. *The First Work.   Until the Cross*

A study of this paragraph will at once reveal the fact of difference between the first work of the apostles and that to which they were ultimately appointed. Here we are first impressed by the limitation of the sphere of their operations. They were forbidden to go to the Gentiles or to the

Samaritans, and were sent to the lost sheep of the house of Israel. The nature of their work was first that of declaring the Kingdom of heaven to be at hand, and secondly that of the power of their Lord by wonders and signs.

The method of their work was to be that of making no provision for their material need ; that of seeking the hospitality of such as were worthy in the cities to which they went ; and that of offering the alternative of peace or judgment to houses and cities, according to whether they were received or not.

While there are underlying principles which abide even to-day, the order of Christian service is now entirely changed, both as to its sphere, its nature, and its method.

2. *The second Period of Service. " Till the Son of Man be come "*

Looking ahead, the King foresaw a day when these men would go forth into the midst of perils which He likened to that of being as sheep in the midst of wolves. That day of peril did not come for the disciples until after the Cross. It is singularly noticeable that all hostility centred upon the King Himself while He was still with them, but after His departure the whole force of it broke upon these men. In view of that time of peril, He declared to them in a brief and suggestive word that the necessary qualifications would be that they should be wise as serpents and harmless as doves. This declaration He followed by warnings and instructions, bidding them first to beware of men, and foretelling their sufferings. He charged them however not to be anxious, because in that day the Spirit of the Father would speak in them, an evident reference to the time of ministry following Pentecost. Moreover it would be a time of division in households, and of persecution for them, during which they were to pass from city to city ; and He declared that they would not have gone over the cities of Israel until He came, this being an evident reference to His coming in judgment, which was fulfilled in the fall of Jerusalem.

3. *The third Period. To the End of the Age*

Looking still forward, the King described a new period of service, in which the supreme note would be that of their identification with Himself. Throughout all that remained of the charge, He spoke of those who would serve Him as disciples, thus recognising that the hour would come when the apostolic work of the twelve would be carried on by a succession of disciples. He spoke first of their identification with Him in misunderstanding. As the Master of the house had been called Beelzebub, so also would the servants.

He then urged them to identification with Him in testimony. He would still speak to them in the darkness, but they were to make proclamation of what He said in the light. In such testimony they were to have no fear of those who would kill the body, but to have perfect confidence in the protection of their Father; and He declared that those who would thus confess Him before men, He would confess before His Father.

He then spoke of their identification with Him in suffering. His coming would inevitably issue in a process not of peace but a sword, in which a man's foes would be they of his own household. In that period they would be called into identification with Him in the bearing of the cross, and would enter into His experience of losing life in order to find it.

Finally He spoke of their identification with Him in His victory. Their reception by men would be His reception; and ministry to them in the midst of their service, He would count as ministry to Himself.

ii. His Difficulties

Having made an end of commanding His twelve disciples, the King Himself departed to preach and teach in their cities, that is, in the cities of these disciples ; and Matthew has recorded a series of events which occurred in that period when He was exercising this ministry during their absence. These stories reveal in a peculiarly graphic way the difficulties which He encountered. In the paragraph we have revealed ; the difficulty and the perplexity of the loyal-hearted ; that of the unreasonableness of the generation ; that of the impenitence of the cities ; and the attitude of Christ in the midst of these difficulties.

a. THE PERPLEXITY OF THE LOYAL. THE BAPTIST

Evidently perplexed by the method which Jesus was adopting, as the question of His disciples on a former occasion indicated, by the absence of fasting, and of those ascetic practices which had been the habit of the forerunner, John sent to ask whether Jesus was indeed the Messiah.

The King's answer was twofold. He first bade the messengers of John recount to him the things which they had seen, the work that was actually being done ; and uttered the word of gentle rebuke, " Blessed is he that shall not be offended in Me."

Having thus answered the messengers, He turned to the multitudes, and challenged them concerning John, as to what had been the reason of their going forth to hear him ; declaring that he was more than a prophet, and that no greater than he had been born of women. He then proceeded to reveal the difficulty in the mind of John as He declared that " The Kingdom of heaven suffereth violence, and men of violence take it by force," by which He recognised the fact that the methods He was adopting were so contrary to all pre-conceived notions as to the way of a King, that men would only enter His Kingdom as

they did violence to their prejudices, and
submitted themselves to Him; or as He
had said to John, were not offended in
Him. The incident is an illustration of a
difficulty confronting the King even in the
case of devout souls.

b. THE UNREASONABLENESS OF MEN.   THE
      GENERATION

Continuing His discourse, the King
complained of the unreasonableness of the
generation, and in His complaint revealed
another difficulty. He used the illustration of children playing in the market-
places, dissatisfied because their fellows
would neither dance to their music, nor
mourn to their wailing.

He then immediately applied His own
illustration as He declared that they had
been dissatisfied with the method of John,
and were dissatisfied with His own method.
The method of John had been that of the
ascetic. He came neither eating nor
drinking, that is, he declined to take any

141

part in their merriment, to dance to their piping. Of him they had said, "He hath a demon." The method of the Son of man was that of comradeship with men. He came eating and drinking, that is, He refused any sympathy with the things which were grieving them. He would not mourn to their wailing, and they said of Him that He was "a gluttonous man, and a winebibber."

His answer to the unreasonableness of His generation was declared in His statement that "Wisdom is justified by her works." There was a wisdom in the asceticism of John, in that he refused to dance, because their music was out of harmony with the Divine joy. There was a wisdom in the method of the Son of man in that He refused to mourn, because their wailing was in the presence of superficial things, and they lacked sorrow for the deepest.

c. THE IMPENITENCE OF THE CITIES.   CHORA-
ZIN.   BETHSAIDA.   CAPERNAUM

The next difficulty is revealed in the
King's upbraiding of the cities in the midst
of which He had exercised His ministry.
His cause of complaint was that they repented not.   Woes were pronounced upon
Chorazin and Bethsaida, in view of the fact
that they had had the opportunities of seeing
His mighty works; and He declared that
had Tyre and Sidon had such opportunities,
they would have repented; and foretold
their doom.

In sternest words He declared that
Capernaum should go down to Hades, for
her wickedness was greater than that of
Sodom, in that her opportunity had been
greater.   Hence her doom was sealed.

d. THE ATTITUDE OF CHRIST IN THE MIDST
OF DIFFICULTIES

In a wonderful paragraph we have a
revelation of the calm strength and restfulness of the King in the midst of the

difficulties which have been revealed. That is first manifest in His adoration, revealing as it does His perfect rest in God; and in the fact that while the things of His Kingdom are hidden from the wise and understanding, they are yet revealed to babes. This adoration was His assent to that very principle which had caused perplexity to John.

The word of adoration was immediately followed by that of proclamation, in which He declared that His authority had been received from His Father, and that while men did not understand Him, His Father did, and that while men did not know the Father, He knew Him.

That word of proclamation merged immediately into the gracious invitation, in which the King called those whom He had seen distressed and scattered, such as laboured and were heavy laden, to Himself, the one true King and Shepherd; in order that they might be restored to God and find rest.

That final word of invitation is most

perfectly understood when we interpret it in the light of this whole section. The perplexed yet loyal-hearted soul in prison, the foolish and unreasonable age, the unrepentant cities in spite of His mighty works; all might find the rest they needed, if they would come to Him, take His yoke, and learn of Him.

iii. His Conflict

We now come to Matthew's particular account of the King's enforcement of His claims in conflict with His adversaries. The section reveals a growth of opposition in four stages, separated from each other by accounts of the continuation of His beneficent ministry.

a. FIRST ATTACKS

We have first the account of three definite attacks upon the King; the first, concerning the Sabbath; the second, concerning His power; and the third, concerning a sign.

1. *Concerning the Sabbath*

Apparently in the same day two attacks were made upon the King concerning His attitude toward the Sabbath; the first in the corn-fields, as He passed through them with His disciples; and the second in the synagogue, in the hour of assembly.

a. *In the Corn-fields*

Passing through the corn-fields the dis-

147

ciples who were hungry, satisfied their
hunger by plucking the ears of corn and
eating; and were immediately criticised for
so doing by the Pharisees. To the criticism
the King replied in defence of His disciples,
first by the use of two illustrations, those of
David and the priests, in which He proved
that under certain circumstances the techni-
cal law of the Sabbath had been set aside
in the interests of human need, without any
violation of the principle involved in the
Sabbath. His final defence of His disciples
however was that of the claim which He
uttered; that He was greater than the
temple, that He desired mercy, and that He
was Lord of the Sabbath.

β. *In the Synagogue*

Upon His arrival in the synagogue, the
Pharisees, with the subject of the Sabbath
still in their minds, and immediately as-
sociating the King with a man who was
present, having a withered hand, challenged
Him as to whether it was lawful to heal on
the Sabbath day.

He first suggested to them a personal question as to whether if their property were in danger on the Sabbath, they would rescue it. He then emphatically declared that because a man was of more value than a sheep, it is lawful to do good on the Sabbath day; and finally He gave them the active answer of restoring the man.

This issued in the plotting of the Pharisees for His death, which Jesus perceiving, He withdrew, but was followed by multitudes whom in grace He healed.

Matthew draws attention to the fact that by this action He fulfilled the prophecy of Isaiah, which declared that the Messiah would neither strive nor cry; that He would take no action of judgment against such as were opposing Him, until He should send forth judgment unto victory.

2. *Concerning His Power*

The next attack upon the King concerned His power. Its occasion was that of His healing of a demoniac ; and the consequent inquiry of the multitude, " Is this the Son of David ? " which of course meant, Is this the Messiah ?

It was in answer to that inquiry that the Pharisees now boldly affirmed that the power by which He wrought these wonders over demons was that of Beelzebub, the prince of the demons. It was a grave and awful charge, and the answer of the King was characterised by great solemnity.

He first exposed the folly of their suggestion as He declared that division within a kingdom means desolation. He then appealed to the witness of their own sons who had cast out demons, and proceeded to declare the alternative to their suggestion. That alternative was that He cast out demons by the Spirit of God, that He cast out demons by having bound the strong man, that is, having gained the victory over

151

Satan. It was in that connection that He uttered the familiar words, " He that is not with Me is against Me ; and he that gathereth not with Me scattereth," which being considered in its relation to this action, will be seen, in its first application to them, to mean that not He, but the men who were opposing Him, were doing the work of Beelzebub.

He then proceeded to utter perhaps the most solemn warning that ever fell from His lips concerning the sin that has no forgiveness. These men had not committed it, for their words were words of blasphemy against the Son of man, which He said should be forgiven. But they were in grave peril of such sin, for He knew that the special ministry which the Spirit would fulfil would be one concerning Himself ; and whereas men might refuse His voice, to refuse Him when finally presented to them by the Spirit would be to sin the sin that can have no forgiveness. After the warning He appealed to them for consistency. They had declared that His beneficent work was the result of complicity with Satan. This was impossible. Let them be consistent, and consent that the good fruit had come from a good tree; or that the things He had done were evil things, because they had come from a corrupt tree.

Having made this appeal, He exposed the impossibility of such honesty on their part as He said, "Ye offspring of vipers, how can ye, being evil, speak good things?" and then proceeded solemnly to warn them against speech unconsidered or dishonest. Speech, He declared, is from the heart, and if men speak idle words, of these they shall give account, for the words of men will justify or condemn them.

3. *Concerning a Sign*

Willing perhaps to be away from the suggestion which they had made in view of the solemnity and sternness of His reply, certain of the Scribes and Pharisees asked Him for a sign.

The answer of the King to the request was characterised by the same severity and solemnity, which had been evident in His previous dealing with them. Speaking of these men as representing their age, He described it as evil and adulterous, and declared that no sign should be given, save the sign of Jonah, and that sign fulfilled in Himself. It was a word which did not constitute an immediate sign to these men, for how could they comprehend it? In effect He declared that the only sign that would be granted would be that of His death and resurrection.

He then proceeded to utter words in condemnation of the generation, declaring that it would be condemned by the men of Nineveh who had been obedient to the

sign of Jonah; while the age in which
He stood was unrepentant in the presence
of a Greater than Jonah. He declared
that the queen of the South would condemn the age, for she had travelled far to
hear the wisdom of Solomon; whereas His
age was opposing Him, rather than listening to His teaching, notwithstanding the
fact that He was greater than Solomon.

Finally He uttered a prophecy concerning the age, of singular solemnity.
This He introduced by an illustration,
that of the restless spirit of evil ejected
from his tenement, seeking rest and finding
none, presently returning to the tenantless
house and finding it swept and garnished,
taking with him seven other spirits more
evil than himself.

The impact of His application must
have been terrific. "Even so shall it be
also unto this evil generation." He thus
described the generation as swept and
garnished, but tenantless. It was a
peculiarly searching criticism of the effect
of the traditionalism of the Pharisees, which

while maintaining a certain correctness of external morality, was devoid of that possession by Jehovah which alone could deliver the age from the ravages of evil. His declaration was that as the last state of the demon-possessed man was worse than the first, so the last state of the generation would be worse than the first. The subsequent history of the national refusal of Christ when proclaimed by the Spirit through His disciples, fulfilled the solemn prophecy to the letter.

His Propaganda

There now followed an interval in the midst of this period characterised by conflict, and it was an interval of teaching in which the King gave utterance to remarkable words concerning kinship with Himself; and gave detailed teaching concerning the processes of His Kingdom.

1. *Concerning Kinship*

It was while He was uttering the solemn words to the multitudes which we considered in our last chapter that His mother and His brethren came, desiring to speak to Him. Matthew does not explain the reason of their coming, but we may gain some light upon it from Mark's account, from which we learn that they had come as the result of a conviction that He was beside Himself.

The King made their coming the occasion of declaring the law of true kinship with Himself. He Who demands that we shall make Him first in our affection, dearer

159

than father or mother or wife or child, declares that those who do so are more to Him than those united by the bonds of earthly relationship, save as they also do the will of God. It has been wrongly imagined by some that the language of the King indicated some reflection upon His mother, as though she had grieved Him; but this is surely to miss the deepest truth in the statement which is not that He loved her less, but those more than earthly kin, who were related to Him by the closer spiritual bond of devotion to the will of God.

2. *Concerning the Kingdom*

To have followed the King through the processes of His ministry until this point will be to understand more perfectly the teaching which He now gave concerning His Kingdom. The whole mission had been beneficent in its intention, but surrounded by difficulty, and characterised by conflict. As we have seen more than once, His methods were not those of

human policy, or such as could be apprehended by those unfamiliar with His own
secret. The Kingdom He had come to
establish must have spiritual foundation,
and it is evident by all that has gone
before, that the victory will only be
realised through processes of conflict and
of contradiction, in which evil must work
itself out to complete manifestation ere
it can be finally cast out. In the teaching concerning the Kingdom the King
set these facts forth in parabolic form.
The teaching may be divided into two
parts; that given in the presence of the
multitude by the sea side; and secondly
that given to the disciples only in the
house.

a. *By the Sea Side*

Making a boat His seat of authority,
while the multitudes stood round Him on
the beach, He uttered first the parable of
the sower, which reveals the first method
of the Kingdom, that of the enunciation of
truth, and its incarnation in the lives of

those who hear it, in order to the bringing forth of the harvest.

Having uttered this first parable His disciples asked Him why He spoke to the people in parabolic form, and He answered them by declaring that He adopted the form because of the blindness of the people, and consequently in fulfilment of prophecy; ending the answer by declaring the blessedness of the disciples in that they both saw and heard what others did not perceive. A careful reading of this explanation will correct a generally accepted misapprehension that Christ spoke in parables, in order that these people might not understand. The reverse is true. Not for mystification, but for simplicity and illustration did He so teach. The word "lest" is a quotation from Isaiah, and refers to the degradation which caused blindness, not to the parables as causing blindness. They closed their eyes lest they should see. Therefore His parabolic teaching was a gracious attempt to reach them by arousing their curiosity.

Having answered the inquiry of His

disciples, He then gave an explanation of the parable of the sower which reveals the fact that the parable has a double application. In the last analysis the seed of the Kingdom is the Word of God, which sown in the individual life and there becoming fruitful, that life in itself is a seed, planted in the age, bringing forth fruit toward the realisation of the Kingdom. Both in the case of the implanting of the Word in the individual, and in that of the planting of the individual in the age, the quantity of the harvest depends upon the quality of the soil. That which is supreme in the parable is the revelation of the fact that the effect of this sowing is not the transformation of all men everywhere and in all ages, to the pattern of the Kingdom. The result is always dependent upon the the one who hears, and how he hears.

He then uttered His second parable, that which revealed the fact that an enemy sows darnel in the same field with the wheat, darnel being characterised by its likeness to wheat in the earlier stages of its growth. That sowing He declared to be the work of an enemy, and that it must go forward until harvest; when the reapers of the true Master of the field would gather both wheat and darnel, separating in the gathering, the darnel for destruction, and the wheat for the barn.

The third parable was that of the mustard seed, which being less than all seeds, yet in process of time became a great tree, so that the birds of the heaven lodged in the branches of it. Nothing is said in the parable as to the nature of the tree, but it is to be observed that the growth described is abnormal, and contrary to Nature.

The fourth parable was that of leaven hidden in three measures of meal so that the whole became leavened. All the quantities are needed for an understanding of the parable; not leaven alone, but leaven in meal, and the effect it produces.

This was the last parable spoken in public, and at the close it is again stated that Jesus spoke in parables to the multitudes, and without a parable said nothing to them, in fulfilment of the word of Isaiah. The word here quoted is a twofold declaration, first the determination to speak in parables; and secondly, the determination by that means to utter things hidden.

β. *In the House*

Having retired to the house with His disciples, the King in answer to their request explained to them the parable of the darnel. There is another sowing going on in the world's broad fields, side by side with that of the Son of man. It is the sowing of the devil. The hour of triumph thereover, the final mastery of evil, does not occur during the period of sowing, but in the time of harvest, which the King distinctly stated will be at the consummation of the age. The character of the age is thus clearly revealed as one of mixture. Separation and the final casting out of evil are the work of a dispensation yet to come. A slight distinction, yet of importance, occurs in the opening part of the parable. "A *man* sowed good seed"; the mischief

b. INCREASING OPPOSITION

After this interval of teaching the King is seen again facing opposition, and two illustrations are given, that of the men of Nazareth, and that of Herod.

1. *The Men of Nazareth*

Returning to His own country, and evidently to His own city of Nazareth, the King entered into the synagogue and taught.

The effect produced upon the men of Nazareth was that first of astonishment. This astonishment was the outcome of the wisdom of His teaching, and the might of the works which He wrought. That which perplexed them was the fact that they imagined they knew everything about Him. They spoke of Him as the carpenter's son, and referred to His mother Mary, to His brethren whom they named, James, and Joseph, and Simon, and Judas; and to His sisters, inquiring, "Are they not all with us? Whence then hath this man all

169

these things ? " The effect of their criticism
was illogical, but human. " They were
offended in Him."

The effect their attitude produced on the
King is revealed in His complaint, " A
prophet is not without honour, save in his
own country, and in his own house "; and
in the declaration of Matthew that " He did
not many mighty works there because of
their unbelief."

2. *Herod*

A new danger threatened in the person
of Herod. The fame of Jesus reached the
palace of the tetrarch, and filled him with
terror. His declaration to his servants is a
revelation of that terror. He imagined that
John the Baptist was risen from the dead.

In this connection Matthew tells the
story of Herod's relation to John, in explanation of the terror which filled him
when the report concerning Jesus reached
him. He had imprisoned John, because
John had protested against his incestuous
affection for the wife of his brother. This

action on the part of Herod is seen to have been the more dastardly in view of a fact which Matthew does not record, but which is found in the Gospel of Mark, that Herod knew that he was a righteous man and a holy, and that in the past he had heard him, and that gladly. Evidently at some period he had passed under the influence of John's preaching, and had been affected toward good thereby. In spite of these things he had imprisoned him, but at first dare not slay him, because he feared the multitude.

There had come a day however, when in the midst of debauch he had taken an oath to give to the child of his paramour anything that she asked; and when the base demand was made for the head of the prophet, he had been guilty of the unholy deed of his murder.

Now when news reached him of the wonders wrought by Jesus, his guilty soul was filled with terror, as the very superstition of his nature suggested to him that the man whom he had murdered, had come back.

When the King knew that the report of
Him had reached Herod, and that Herod
was filled with terror, He withdrew to the
desert; for in the case of such a man as
Herod, craven fear would be the inspiration
of a dastardly courage which would stop
at nothing, in order to accomplish its ends.

It is very interesting to note how constantly the Lord acted on the basis of a
true caution in the presence of threatened
peril, notwithstanding the fact that in other
connections He constantly declared that
men could have no power over Him until
His hour was come.

(*b*) AN INTERVAL OF BENEFICENT ACTIVITY

Having thus withdrawn to the desert, multitudes followed Him on foot from the cities; and far removed from those who were hostile to Him, there followed another interval in which He exerted His power in beneficent ministry. There are three stories of the exercise of that ministry; those of the feeding of the multitudes; the stilling of the storm; and a great ministry of healing.

1. *The Feeding of the Multitudes*

Coming forth from His seclusion, He saw the crowds that had followed Him, and the vision of them again moved His heart with compassion, which He expressed by healing their sick.

As the shadows of the evening fell, the disciples besought Him to send the people away, in order that they might provide themselves with food.

The answer of the King was an exercise of His Kingly authority and power in feed-

ing the multitudes. First declaring that
there was no need that they should go
away, He commanded His disciples to feed
them. Naturally they immediately thought
of their resources, and emphasised their
insufficiency.

Taking the little they had, the King
multiplied, while the disciples distributed to
the crowds. Thus in the desert He exercised His power in healing the sick, and
feeding with five loaves and two fishes, five
thousand men, besides women and children.
We are astonished that men did not believe
on Him when they saw such wondrous
works wrought by His hands. Yet is not
the unbelief of to-day more astonishing,
for on every hand He is accomplishing
the greater works of spiritual feeding and
healing, and yet men do not believe.

2. *The Stilling of the Storm*

Having satisfied His own heart by
satisfying the need of the crowd, the
King sent His disciples before Him to
the other side of the sea; and then dis-

missing the crowds, retired to a mountain for loneliness and prayer. It is of great interest to see that even He felt the need of escaping at times from the multitudes. The only way in which it is possible to keep near to the crowds in all highest and tenderest senses, is to get away from them at times into loneliness with God. Such hours of communion with the Eternal Love are the hours that keep us compassionate in the presence of human need. Familiarity with the crowd produces hardening. Familiarity with God issues in a perpetual re-sensitising of the heart, which prevents hardening.

While the King was thus in the quiet restfulness of communion with God, the disciples were beset by difficulty. A storm had arisen, lashing the waves into fury, and the wind was contrary.

The Master in His place of quiet retirement had not forgotten these men ; and in the moment of their gravest peril He came to them over the sea and through the wind, strong to deliver, and mighty to save. Their fear of the storm was forgotten in their terror at what appeared to them to be a phantom, moving across the troubled waters toward them, until they heard the well-known voice, " Be of good cheer; it is I ; be not afraid." It was in that moment of revelation that Peter made his great venture of faith, and successfully walked upon the waters, until consciousness of the circumstances, making him for a moment forgetful of the power of his Lord, he began to sink. The grace of the Master was immediately revealed in the fact that when the cry of the sinking man was heard, He stretched forth His hand to succour him, rebuking not the venture of his faith, but the doubt which had made it fail.

The issue of these manifestations of the power of the King was that the disciples in the boat worshipped Him, and declared that in truth He was the Son of God.

3. *The Ministry of Healing*

The last of these three stories is briefly

178

told, and yet it is full of revelation. When the men of Gennesaret knew Him, they gathered from the whole region those that were sick, and asked that they might be allowed only to touch the border of His garment. It is evident that the King granted them their request, for Matthew briefly declares " As many as touched were made whole."

C. RENEWED ATTACK

The interval of quietness was broken in upon by a renewed attack, the story of which is mainly occupied with the remarkable and searching answer of the King. We have in this story the account of the coming of the deputation; of the King's answer to them; and of His explanation of that answer to the multitude, and then to His disciples.

1. *The Jerusalem Deputation*

A company of Pharisees and scribes from Jerusalem now came to the King with a definite complaint, which they uttered in the form of a question. The question they raised was not one of cleanliness, but one of ritual. The washing of hands for the removal of imaginary evil was a part of the tradition of the elders. To read the inquiry to-day is to be impressed with its triviality, and yet that very triviality reveals the straits in which these men found themselves, in order to formulate any charge against the King.

2. *The King's Answer*

That the question involved more than appears to us is evident from the passionate protest uttered by the King in answer to the inquiry. It was a protest against the evil of tradition. He declared first that tradition transgressed the commandment of God. Of this He gave these men an immediate and pertinent illustration. He first quoted a commandment, "Honour thy father and thy mother," and a commentary upon that from the Mosaic code, "He that speaketh evil of father or mother, let him die the death." He then quoted one of their own traditions which permitted the neglect of father and mother in the supposed interest of religion. That illustration revealed the fact that tradition makes void the law of God.

He then uttered a severe word of denunciation as He called them hypocrites, and declared that Isaiah's prophecy was fulfilled in them, that they were the people who honoured God with the lips, while their heart was far from Him ; in that their worship of Him was vain because they taught the precepts of men.

3. *The King's Explanation*

His estimate of the seriousness of the question which had been asked is further demonstrated by the fact that having thus replied to the deputation, He called the multitude to Him, and explained His protest against tradition in the words, " Not that which entereth into the mouth defileth the man ; but that which proceedeth out of the mouth, this defileth the man." This was a word having bearing on the actual question they had asked about the neglect of washing of the hands in the eating of bread. Nothing that a man takes into his physical being by such action can defile the man. Those things which proceed out of the mouth, such things as the Pharisees themselves had uttered, are the things that defile. Not that they defile in the act of being uttered; but that they, in their utterance, demonstrate a condition of defilement.

The disciples then approached Him, having evidently seen that His answer had angered the Pharisees, inquiring, " Knowest Thou that the Pharisees were offended, when they heard this saying ? " and His answer revealed the fact that what He had said was of supreme importance, whether the Pharisees were offended or not. The tendency of human nature has ever been to make a religion of outward observances ; what a man eats or drinks, or whether he does this, or neglects to do that. These are supposed to be the criteria of his acceptance with God. Such views the King ruthlessly swept on one side as He re-affirmed the teaching of the mount, that character is supreme. The law of God is only perfect as it stands alone. The addition of human tradition imposes unwarranted burdens, and when men try to carry these, they do so at the cost of laying down the true burden of the Divine Will. Tradition is a plant of human planting. Let it then be rooted up, no matter how venerable it is, or how men may be offended by the process. Moreover, He declared that they need have no care about these Pharisees, and charged them to let them alone, for they were blind guides.

Evidently not having grasped the full meaning of the Master's teaching, Peter asked an explanation of what the King had said to the multitudes. Gently rebuking him, the King gave a detailed explanation of His meaning, as He declared that the things that come forth from the heart are evil thoughts, murders, adulteries, fornications, thefts, false witness, railings ; affirming that by such things men are defiled, and not by eating with unwashen hands.

Him to send her away, by which they did not mean to suggest that He should dismiss her without granting her request, but that He should give her what she asked, and so be rid of her. This is evident from the King's answer, in which He declared that He was not sent except to the lost sheep of the house of Israel.

It was then that the woman's persistence was most wonderfully manifested. Pressing nearer to Him, she fell in reverence before Him, and cried out of the depth of her heart, " Lord, help me "; and in answer the King said what at first appears to be one of the most unusual things that ever fell from His lips. " It is not meet to take the children's bread and cast it to the dogs." To this apparent rebuff the woman replied, by agreeing, and yet urging that there was a privilege which even dogs might enjoy, that of the crumbs which fall from the masters' table. To that appeal the King immediately answered in a word of high commendation, and in a deed of healing power.

His Propaganda

How strange at first this story is in the matter of the silence of the King, and then of His rebuff. The reason of His attitude is revealed in the result which followed. He knew how strong that woman's faith was, and His method was one which resulted in the manifestation of that faith in all its beauty. How perpetually the very best of character is hidden, until for its forthshining the King hides His face. It is in the darker dispensations of His dealings with us that we learn the meaning of His method, and so discover Him most perfectly. It is through such circumstances moreover, that we are changed into His likeness, and our best and highest possibilities are realised. When He seems least kind, let us rest assured that His lovingkindness is most perfectly at work, and let us then most patiently wait for Him.

2. *The Ministry of Healing*

In this story of the gathering of the multitudes to Him on the mountain in Galilee, bringing with them their impotent

189

d. ALLIED HOSTILITY

The final movement in this section specially dealing with the conflict of the King,
tells the story of a formal request for a sign
preferred by a coalition of Pharisees and
Sadducees. We have the account of the
demand for a sign; the answer of the King;
and His explanation of His answer to His
own disciples.

1. *The Demand for a Sign*

That which is remarkable in this attack
upon Christ was the fact that the deputation was composed of representatives of the
two religious parties most utterly opposed.
It was a coalition of men holding entirely
divergent views, for the express purpose
of leading Him into some attempt which
would in their opinion have revealed His
incompetence. The form of their request
would seem to suggest that for the moment
they admitted that He had wrought signs
on the earth, but they now asked for one

from heaven ; that is, something patently supernatural and spectacular.

2. *The Answer of the King*

The King's response consisted of rebuke and refusal. He first rebuked them for the fact that they were wise in the matter of the weather, but entirely lacking wisdom in the spiritual signs of the times.

He then definitely refused to give the sign they asked, giving as His reason that the sign was asked in the name of an evil and adulterous generation ; briefly repeating what He had said with greater definiteness on a previous occasion, that the only sign that would be granted to them would be that of Jonah. There is nothing more interesting in the story of this propaganda of the King than His suppression of the marvellous powers which He possessed. How easily He might have given these men a sign which would have startled and overwhelmed them. But He never used His power save in the realm of the Divine wisdom and love. Any mere exhibition of

194

ability would have been wasted so far as the purpose of His life and ministry, that of the establishment of the Kingdom of heaven, was concerned. There is no waste in the economy of Jesus. His pearls are never cast before swine.

3. *The Explanation to His Disciples*

As the direct outcome of this request for a sign, and His refusal, He uttered words of solemn warning to His disciples. Matthew introduces his record of this warning by briefly noticing the fact that His disciples had forgotten to take bread, thus preparing us for a misunderstanding on their part, to be almost immediately described. The King's warning consisted of the command to beware of the leaven of the Pharisees and Sadducees, by which as a subsequent declaration reveals, He warned them against the teaching of these men. Traditionalism and naturalism are corrupting influences in religion.

The disciples did not understand Him. Their sense of difficulty is revealed in the statement that they reasoned among themselves, and the result of the reasoning was that they decided that He referred to the fact that they had not brought bread. It is an amazing revelation of the blindness of these men. It really appears as though the two miracles of feeding had impressed them with the importance of taking loaves, rather than that of being with Christ. Thus are men constantly in danger of putting the emphasis in the wrong place.

Knowing their difficulty, and their false decision, the Lord gave them an explanation of His meaning, as He first rebuked them for their lack of faith, and, reminding them of the miracles, declared that He had not spoken concerning bread. He then repeated His word of warning, leaving them to come to a right understanding of His intention, seeing that He had now eliminated the fact of their concern about loaves. Matthew declares that they then understood that He spoke not of the leaven of bread, but of the teaching of the Pharisees and Sadducees.

iv. His Victory

This is the last movement in the section
dealing with the King's enforcement of
claims, and brief though the paragraph be,
it is of the greatest importance, for it tells
the story of that victory which prepared
the way for the final movement in His
mission.

By the persistent and clearly manifested
action of the rulers the King had now been
rejected, and consequently the establishment of the Kingdom was postponed. Here
we have the first hint of a new departure.
Matthew records the challenge of the King,
and the confession of the disciples; and the
confession of the King, and His charge to
His disciples.

a. THE CHALLENGE AND CONFESSION

Having arrived in the parts of Cæsarea
Philippi He challenged them as to who men
said that He was. They replied in such
a way as to reveal the singular effect which
His ministry had produced, telling Him

199

only of the highest and best things they had heard. Their testimony revealed the fact that in His ministry, men had detected the true prophetic note, and that, in varied emphases ; as they had spoken of Him as John the Baptist, Elijah, Jeremiah, or one of the prophets.

Having heard this statement the King immediately narrowed and intensified His inquiry as He appealed to them " But who say ye that I am ? " It was in answer to that inquiry that Simon Peter made his great confession, a confession of conviction that his Master was indeed the Christ, the Son of the living God, or in other words, that He was the long looked for Messiah, the King for Whom the nation had been waiting. There is no reason to doubt that on this occasion, as was so constantly the case, Peter was the spokesman for the rest of the disciples. This then was the supreme hour up to this point, of the victory in the ministry of the Lord. In order that He might proceed to the completion of His work in the world, it was necessary that there should be those who were more than loyal to Him as a great Teacher, sympathetic with Him as a great Idealist, or impressed by Him as a mighty Worker. They must at least realise His separation from all other teachers, and that He was the supreme One in that economy of God, in which they had been born. This victory was achieved, Peter's confession being the evidence thereof.

b. THE CONFESSION AND CHARGE

The King immediately responded to the confession of Peter as He uttered the word of blessing upon him, declaring that what he had now confessed had not been revealed to him by flesh and blood, but by His Father. The revelation had come to the man through Christ Himself, not merely through the perfection and power of His human influence, but because the Father had been able through the Son to express the fulfilment of His purpose in Him.

Having thus uttered His beatitude, He made His great confession, and revealed the

C. HIS PASSION

We now come to final division of the Gospel, the one at once most full of majesty and mystery. It was a period during which His own disciples were unable to understand Him fully. They were filled with amazement and dread, and walked after Him rather than with Him. All the way He was patiently dealing with them, persistently leading them into the neighbourhood of the Cross, and preparing them both for the darkness of the final hour, and for the dawning of a new day of illumination, in which they would understand as they could not at the moment, the things He did and said. For the most part His ministry was exercised on their behalf from Cæsarea Philippi to Calvary. Not that He entirely abandoned the multitudes, for again and again He turned to them, and to the end manifested His compassion toward them. There are four sections in the division dealing with; His Cross and His subjects; His rejection of the Hebrew nation; His prediction to His subjects; and His travail and triumph.

I. HIS CROSS AND HIS SUBJECTS

After Cæsarea Philippi the King devoted Himself in a very special way to the instruction of His subjects concerning the Cross; and a careful consideration of the whole section will reveal three movements dealing with three aspects of the Cross. The first was concerned with the Cross and the glory; the second with the Cross and the grace; the third with the Cross and the Kingdom. In each of these we shall find first definite instruction, and then some form of illustration, in the doing and teaching of the King.

i. THE CROSS AND THE GLORY
a. INSTRUCTION

Immediately following the confession of Peter, and the King's answering confession concerning His Church, He began to speak of His Cross. Whereas there are evidences of His own consciousness of that Cross in the earlier stages of His ministry, and figurative allusions to it, He had never definitely referred to it until this period. The first unveiling was characterised by an almost awful directness of statement, as He told them that He must go to Jerusalem, suffer many things of the rulers, be killed, and the third day be raised up. Let it at once be observed that His statement concerning the Cross included the declaration of resurrection.

From this unveiling of the Cross His disciples instinctively shrank. They were as yet only subjects of the King, interpreting Kingship according to their own ideals. The wisdom and the love of God were beyond their comprehension, and therefore they trembled, and Peter became the spokesman of their protest. That protest was passionate and angry. There can be no question that it was born of his affection for his Lord, and his conviction that what He proposed, was the utterest folly in the interest of the establishment of the Kingdom.

The King immediately explained His

meaning in the most startling and arresting way. He sternly rebuked the attitude of Peter as He addressed him as Satan, and declared that his mental attitude was out of harmony with the Divine purpose, and accorded with the materialised outlook of men.

He then clearly declared that those who would follow Him henceforth must in the necessity of the case do so by the way of the Cross, and that the only preparation for such following would be the denial of self, and fellowship in the Cross; appealing to them in the words which have become solemnly familiar, " What shall a man be profited, if he shall gain the whole world, and forfeit his life ? or what shall a man give in exchange for his life ? "

Closely connected with this first unveiling of the Cross the King made proclamation of the coming glory, as He declared that He would come in glory, and that in such coming would render to men according to their works. The last word was that of a promise that some of those who listened

should yet see Him coming in His Kingdom, an unquestionable reference to the
vision granted them on the holy mount.

b. ILLUSTRATION

This teaching concerning the Cross and
the glory was immediately followed by
the illustration of the holy mount, and
that which followed. On the mount they
had a manifestation of the relation between
the glory and the Cross; and in the valley
an application of the truth.

1. *Manifestation*

"After six days," and it is interesting
to observe that we have no record of what
transpired in those days. In all probability
they were days of silence. The strange
declaration of the King concerning the
Cross had crushed the hearts of these men.

Now, to three of their number, as special
training for special service, was granted a
wondrous vision of His glory. In the high
mountain apart they saw Him in all the
resplendent beauty of His perfected human-

MATT.   209   P

The appeal to the King was made by a father on behalf of his boy, and in the appeal He declared the helplessness of the disciples to whom he had brought the boy.

The answer of the King was first that of rebuke of the generation, and then that of the word of power whereby the demon was sent forth, and the boy was cured.

The disciples immediately asked why they had failed, and were answered that their failure was due to their lack of faith. It was a striking answer. They had failed for lack of that faith which yields the whole life to His control. When the father brought the boy to them, there was in their heart a questioning of Him concerning the last word He had spoken to them, as to the necessity for the Cross; and the presence of that unbelief paralysed their power. They had cast out demons before, but now because of failure of faith they had failed. Hence they were reminded that in this new economy the glory of victory must come by the way of the acceptation of the Cross.

ii. The Cross and the Grace

a. INSTRUCTION

In this section the dominant note is that of the grace which results from the acceptation of the principle of the Cross. We have first the direct teaching of the King, and secondly His indirect revelation of this grace.

1. *Direct*

For a time after the experience of the mount, they remained in Galilee, and there the Lord repeated the declaration which He had made at Cæsarea Philippi concerning His Cross and His resurrection. That they had learned something in the interval is evident from the fact that there was no protest; but that they were still under the shadow is revealed in the statement that they were exceeding sorry.

2. *Indirect*

In the incidents and the teaching immediately following we have the revelation of the grace which results from the Cross. There are three matters to be considered; the Cross and the commonplace; the Cross and greatness; the Cross and forgiveness.

a. *The Cross and the Commonplace*

In Capernaum those who received the half-shekel asked Peter whether their Master paid it. It is evident that they were collecting it, from the fact that subsequently it was paid, as the story reveals. The negative form of their question is suggestive of a critical attitude, as though they did not think that He did pay it. Peter replied that He did.

The reply while perfectly natural and intended in defence of his Lord, was incidentally a revelation of the fact that he did not understand Who his Lord was; and his answer afforded the opportunity for an action on the part of the King, which was a revelation of His grace.

His conversation with Simon suggestively reminded him of His relation to God,

216

which had been proclaimed upon the mountain, and which Peter had confessed at Cæsarea Philippi. Because He was the Son of the King, He was not liable to the paying of tribute. Then immediately His action was a revelation of His grace. In order that these men might not be caused to stumble, He Who was free as Son, consented to bondage, in that He paid the half-shekel. His grace was moreover manifested in the fact that He paid it in fellowship with Peter.

β. *The Cross and Greatness*

The disciples came to Jesus asking, " Who then is greatest in the Kingdom of heaven ? " and the inquiry was a revelation of their inability to understand His teaching concerning the Cross, or to accept it as a principle of life.

The King's answer consisted of an action, and teaching growing out of that action. He first took a child, and set him in the midst, and then keeping their attention fixed upon that child throughout; He brought them face to face with the necessity for the Cross.

They had asked Him as to greatness within the Kingdom. He declared that in order to enter the Kingdom they must become as children, and in order to greatness they must humble themselves as that child. In order to be like the child, they must consent to the principle of the Cross.

Then, His eye still upon the child, He went further, and showed that in order to serve the child, they must consent to the same principle. The possibility of service was first declared, and dignified, as He declared that the reception of the child was the reception of Himself. The peril of failure was revealed in His solemn words concerning the possibility of making a child stumble ; and finally the power by which that peril should be avoided, and that possibility of service realised was declared in the most solemn terms ; and again they were the terms that insisted upon the necessity for consent to the

Cross, even to the point of cutting off of the hand or foot, or the plucking out of the eye.

With the child still as the centre of observation, He further revealed that the way by which the little child might be saved was that of the Cross. He affirmed the Divine interest in the child as He declared that their angels behold the face of the Father in heaven; and then in brief words, adopting the figure of the shepherd, revealed the Divine activity, finally affirming that the Divine purpose was that not one little one should perish. In order therefore to the saving of the child, there must be the method of the Cross in the journey to the mountains to seek that which goeth astray.

γ. *The Cross and Forgiveness*

The grace resulting from the Cross is revealed in the teaching which has to do with forgiveness, and here we have the King's teaching; the inquiry of Peter; and the King's answer thereto.

The King's Teaching

The teaching of the King on this subject commenced with a supposition, " If thy brother sin against thee," and proceeded to reveal the gracious activity of the Cross in such a case.

The motive of everything inculcated is that of the gaining of the brother who has sinned. This is to be attempted by individual approach, and it will at once be recognised that in such approach there is need for the denial of self. If the individual approach fails, then the same purpose is to be aimed at by united appeal. If this should also fail, then the Church is to take action, and it must be remembered that the end sought is still that of the gaining of the sinning brother. This is true moreover, even when the Church, because of his rebellion, is compelled to separate him from its fellowship. He is then to be looked upon as a Gentile and a publican, that is, as a man for whom Christ died, on behalf of whom the Church is to exercise a ministry intended to restore him.

If these instructions are carefully considered, the difficulty of them will at once be recognised ; and that difficulty the King evidently recognised, for it was in this connection that He uttered the remarkable words, setting forth the authority of the Church, revealing the law of prayer by which it is able to exercise that authority, and unveiling the central secret both of prayer and of authority, that of His own presence in the midst. In the light of the whole of this movement it will be seen that the King in the midst is the One, Who according to His own teaching, was to be crowned by the way of the Cross ; and consequently the authority of the Church growing out of fellowship with God through Him, is the authority which she gains in fellowship with His Cross.

Peter's Inquiry

It is evident that the duty of forgiveness was impressed upon the disciples by the fact that Peter asked Him " How oft ? " The question moreover seems to suggest Peter's sense of the difficulty of obedience.

The King's Answer

The answer of the King to Peter was first a direct word. Peter had suggested forgiving seven times, and perhaps imagined that in that suggestion he had reached the ultimate height of virtue. The suggestion of seven was swept away by the King's seventy times seven.

Then He illustrated His teaching by the parable of the king reckoning with his servants. In that parable there is a revelation of the fact that the way of the king was that of compassion, which expressed itself in forgiveness. The way of the forgiven servant was that of lack of compassion, which expressed itself in exacting the utmost. Therefore the way of the king was that of punishing the servant for lack of compassion.

Again the response to Peter was direct as the Master definitely declared that if His disciples did not forgive every one his brother from the heart, neither would God forgive them.

b. ILLUSTRATION

The grace resulting from the Cross is now illustrated in the series of events recorded, and that in four realms ; the physical, the ethical, the social, and the spiritual.

1. *Physical. Healing.*

Immediately after the definite teaching of His disciples in Galilee, the King came into Judæa, and Matthew briefly records the fact that multitudes followed Him, and He healed them there. In an earlier part of his record Matthew, having come to an understanding of this healing ministry before he wrote his Gospel, declared that it was exercised in the power of the Cross, and here, that is to be borne in mind. He was again in Judæa, approaching Jerusalem, going thither as He had said, submitting to the Cross, and that explains Matthew's word, " He healed them *there.*" He was expressing His greatness in service, and exercising forgiveness in compassion.

2. *Ethical.*   *Divorce.*

Again the Pharisees came to Him, and
this time asked Him mostevident ly with
the desire to involve Him in conflict, "Is
it lawful for a man to put away his wife
for every cause?"

That inquiry called forth a very remarkable word from the Master. He first
reminded them that in the Divine economy
from the beginning a man entered the
marriage relationship by the way of the
principle of the Cross. Marriage must
consist of union, by separation from father
and mother, and consequently it becomes
a union indissoluble.

This called forth their second question
as to why, if that were so, Moses had
provided for divorcement.

The King answered that the provision
was made to meet the necessity of their
failure, and then enunciated His own great
law of divorcement, in which He insisted
upon the principle of the Cross as He
declared that there must be no separation

save in the interest of purity, and then it must be complete and abiding.

The disciples' comment reveals their estimate of the severity of the word of the King; and the King's answer to them is a recognition of that severity. They suggested that it was not expedient to marry; and He in effect said to them that if this were so, then by the celibate life in exceptional cases there would be a fulfilment of the principle of the Cross for the sake of the Kingdom of heaven.

3. *Social. Children.*

It is surely more than a coincidence, that immediately following this high teaching, children were brought to Him that He might bless them.

Again the disciples blundered as they rebuked those who brought the children, evidently because they felt that attention to them was beneath the dignity of the King.

The action of the King in response was the action of the grace which results from

the Cross. This expressed itself in anger
with the men who would have driven the
children away ; for while in this case again,
Matthew does not chronicle the fact, Mark
tells us that He spoke, moved with indignation. It then expressed itself as He laid
His hands on the children in blessing.

4. *Spiritual.* *The young Ruler*

As the King passed upon His way, there
came one to Him in quest of eternal life.

To him, the King responded by an
arresting challenge as to why he had come
to Him concerning goodness, and the
declaration that the way into life was the
the way of law.

The ruler immediately asked to which
commandment He made reference, and the
King replied by reciting briefly to him the
laws of human inter-relationship as they
had been enunciated in the old economy.

The young man immediately claimed
that he had been obedient to these laws,
and asked, " What lack I yet ? "

The King then revealed to him the fact

that his surrender to authority was not complete, in that he had never yielded his all; and showed that in order to do so he must follow by the way of the Cross, giving up all that upon which he had depended, and submitting himself entirely to control.

As the disciples were filled with sorrow when the Lord spoke of His Cross, so this young man went away sorrowful, because he had great possessions.

iii. THE CROSS AND THE KINGDOM
a. INSTRUCTION

Matthew now records a series of instructions which the King gave to His disciples, in which the relation between the Cross and the Kingdom is revealed. They have to do with entrance to the Kingdom ; service in the Kingdom ; and positions in the Kingdom.

1. *Entrance to the Kingdom*

The teaching of Jesus on this subject was the result of His dealing with the young man who had gone away sorrowful, for the moment at least refusing to accept the principle of the Cross, and thus declining to enter the Kingdom. The difficulty of entrance in such a case as his was due to the fact that only by the way of the Cross is entrance possible.

While the difficulty was recognised, the possibility was declared. The astonishment of the disciples is a clear revelation of how entirely opposed the mind of man is to this doctrine of the denial of self, and the taking up of the Cross. They could not understand why it should be difficult for a rich man to enter the Kingdom of God. In common with all men, they had taken it for granted that wealth was a passport to all privilege.

The King's answer to their inquiry, " Who then can be saved ? " did not minimise the difficulty, but rather emphasised it as He said, " With men this is impossible." But then in this matter of the Kingdom, men were not dealing with men alone. They had to do with God, and with Him all things are possible, even submission to the Cross in order to enter His Kingdom.

In view of this teaching Peter declared that the disciples had left all to follow Christ, and asked what personal gain would come to them as the result of this action ; and it is to be specially noticed that Christ did not rebuke him for asking this question, but definitely declared that the twelve men who had followed Him under difficult circumstances, should ultimately sit upon twelve thrones, judging the twelve tribes of Israel. He immediately added however that that crown would come to them as the result of their acceptation of the Cross, as they had left the ties of kindred, and the advantages of worldly possession for His name's sake.

His last word was one of warning as He declared that " Many shall be last that are first ; and first that are last."

2. *Service in the Kingdom*

In immediate connection with His de- claration concerning entrance to the King- dom, the King uttered His parable of the labourers in the vineyard, which concludes with the words, " So the last shall be first, and the first last"; showing its relation to the subject in hand. It deals however not so much with the matter of entrance to the Kingdom, as of service within it ; but in its revelation of the true principle of service it explains the necessity for submission to the Cross on the part of

the workers. To such, the reward will not be equal to that of men who have borne the burden and heat of the day.

3. *Positions in the Kingdom*

The King was taking His last journey to Jerusalem, fully conscious of its deep significance in His mission. He was going, as we have seen, of deliberate and set purpose to the Cross. Beyond that Cross He saw the glory of resurrection. On the way He again called His disciples to Him, and in His words to them, and their response to Him we are brought face to face again with a striking contrast between the mind of God and the mind of men; and are thus reminded of His words of rebuke to Peter at Cæsarea Philippi, "Thou mindest not the things of God, but the things of men." He revealed the mind of God in His deliberate and detailed declaration of what He knew would be the issue of His journey to Jerusalem. He was going by the way of the Cross, and that was the way to the crown.

His Passion

Here as in every case during the last sad days, His account of His own coming suffering was broken in upon by a question of precedence among the disciples. The mother of James and John asked that her sons might occupy the positions of power in His coming Kingdom. When we read this story we are tempted to be angry. He was not. He replied by uttering the challenge of the Cross as He spoke of His own coming cup of sorrow, and asked if they were able to drink it. Little understanding the deep meaning of His question they declared that they were; and He immediately accepted the intention of their willingness, and declared that they should indeed drink that cup.

This request for the two resulted in the anger of the ten; and the King gently rebuked this anger by declaring to them again that in His Kingdom greatness would result from service, and quoted His own ministry as the supreme example.

b. ILLUSTRATION

As they moved on their way, in the neighbourhood of Jericho the King gave an illustration of the power which He exercised as the result of His separation to the Cross. He was on His way to the ratification, by actual word and deed, of that which had already taken place in the counsel of the nation; His own rejection as King. On the way two needy men sought a favour from Him as the Son of David, a manner of address that signified their acknowledgment of His Messiahship. The multitude rebuked them, but they were the more persistent in their cry.

Straightway the compassion of the King expressed itself in the exercise of power which answered their prayer, and gave them their sight. To what strange scenes their eyes were opened. One wonders whether during all the tragic and awful events of the succeeding days they continued to follow Him. If so, how inexplicable and mysterious it must have seemed to them, that One Who was able by a touch to open their eyes, should yet be unable to deliver Himself from His foes. This was the supreme mystery to all those who were closely associated with Him, both foes and friends. To-day we know that the power which thrilled through His touch, and communicated vision to sightless eyes, was that which bound Him to the Cross. It was the power of His love.

II. HIS REJECTION OF THE HEBREW NATION

It is very necessary that the whole of this section should be taken into account, as we consider its parts. To move through the story, observing separated incidents only, would be entirely to miss the supreme value of the section, which presents the picture, not of a victim mastered by circumstances, but of a Victor, moving with authority and power through adverse circumstances, which He compelled to the carrying out of His own purpose. We have more than once drawn attention to the fact that He was already rejected by the Hebrew nation. This section gives the account of His official rejection of that nation from its place in the economy of God. There are three movements which we shall consider ; the coming of the King ; the arraignment of the rulers ; and the doom and sentence.

i. The Coming of the King

In the account of the coming of the King

to Jerusalem we have the story of preparation, of entry, and of the executive cleansing of the temple.

a. THE PREPARATION

On their journey toward the city they had arrived at Bethphage, which was situated on the mount of Olives, which was on the east of Jerusalem, and rose to a greater height than mount Zion. From that elevation the King chose to descend to the city. Into the village He sent disciples to bring to Him a colt, that in fulfilment of prophecy He might ride into the city, thus definitely drawing attention to Himself, and calling forth a demonstration.

b. THE KING'S ENTRY

No picture in the life of the King is more full of sadness than this one which we so often describe as the triumphal entry. There can be no question that in the high economy of God it was a triumphal entry, but it was surely a part of the way of sadness for the King. He rode into the city over the garments and the branches of trees which the multitudes spread on His path, and amid acclamations which proclaimed Him Messiah. That the entry was a remarkable one is demonstrated by the fact that all the city was stirred thereby, and as the dwellers within the city gathered together, they inquired "Who is this?" and received the answer from the multitudes, "This is the prophet, Jesus, from Nazareth of Galilee."

c. THE EXECUTIVE CLEANSING

Passing through the city, the King came directly to the temple, and cast out from thence those who were occupied in selling and buying, overthrowing the tables of the money-changers, and the seats of the sellers of doves; as He did so uttering His denunciation of their desecration of the holy place. This was the second time that He had cleansed the temple, and by His action He revealed His conception of the secret of civic righteousness and strength. He had entered the city as the King, and in

doing so He did not find His way to the
governing authority, but to the temple.
This temple He cleansed, and restored it to
its true use, as the blind and the lame
gathered to Him there, and He healed
them, to the accompaniment of the songs
of the children. These songs stirred the
suspicion and anger of the rulers, and they
asked Him, " Hearest Thou what these are
saying ? " In this question they drew
attention to the fact that the children were
proclaiming Him as Messiah, and the
intention of their inquiry was as to whether
He was prepared to accept such honour.
The King's answer was direct and unequivocal as He described the song of the
children as the perfecting of praise.

At the moment His enemies took no
action, and the King left the temple ; and
passing out of the city He went to Bethany,
where He stayed the night.

ii. THE ARRAIGNMENT OF THE RULERS

On the following day the King returned to the city, and there took place His final conflict with the rulers, ending with His official sentence and doom. Matthew's account of these things deals first with a parabolic act of judgment on the way to Jerusalem; and secondly with the King's dealing with the rulers.

a. THE PARABOLIC ACT

On His way to the city, the King performed the only miracle of judgment which He ever wrought, as by a word of command, He destroyed the fig tree, whereon He found nothing but leaves.

This action impressed His disciples, and they inquired " How did the fig tree immediately wither away ? " It is interesting to notice that they did not ask why He destroyed the tree, but how He did it. There is nothing in the story to suggest either that they understood His meaning, or that they did not. I think that it is most probable that they thoroughly understood, but they were perplexed as to the swiftness of the judgment, for we notice that the word *immediately* is twice used, once in Matthew's description of what happened, and once in the inquiry of the disciples.

Moreover He did not give them any explanation of the meaning, but answered the question as they asked it, affirming the power of faith, and the power of prayer, as at their disposal for doing even more wonderful things than they had seen done.

There can however be no doubt that the value of the miracle was parabolic. There has been a good deal of discussion as to this act of the Lord, as though in itself it were out of harmony with strict justice, especially in view of Mark's declaration that " it was not the season of figs." That declaration was evidently literally true, for these things happened in March, and the first fig crop is not gathered until June. On the other hand, the early fruit buds appear on the fig tree in February, and its leaves unfold

in March. On this fig tree the Lord found
nothing but leaves only. It was evident that
there would be no fruit on this tree, because
its vitality had run to leaf. In that it was
a perfect picture of the Jewish nation, and
His judgment on the tree was an equally
perfect symbol of the judgment to fall on
the Jewish nation, as to its reason.

b. THE KING AND THE RULERS

On arrival at the temple there commenced
those events in which the King uttered His
judgments concerning rulers and nation;
and there are four very distinct movements
in the story; those of the King's first
question concerning the herald; the finding
of the verdict against the rulers; the public
unmasking of the rulers; and the King's
final question concerning the Messiah.

1. *The King's first Question. Concerning
the Herald*

As Jesus was teaching in the temple, the
chief priests and elders came to Him, and
openly challenged His authority. He met

251

them by asking them concerning His herald,
whether his baptism was from heaven or
from men. They would not say from
heaven, for they were hypocrites, and knew
that He would charge them with incon-
sistency in that they did not receive him.
They dare not say from men, because they
were cowards, and knew that the multitude
held John as a prophet. Therefore with a
calm dignity, conscious of the fact that He
had already answered them, He refused to
reply in any other form to their question
concerning His authority.

2. *The Finding of the Verdict*

There is hardly any picture in the entire
Gospel more full of dignity, and of the
unerring wisdom of the King than that
which is now presented. He revealed the
failure of the rulers in a series of three
parables, in the first two of which He compelled them to find a verdict against themselves, and in the third revealed the truth
concerning their rejection of the Kingdom
as He had presented it. By the use of

these parables He found a verdict against them as to methods, as to motives, and as to their rejection of the Kingdom.

a. *As to Methods*

The first parable was that of the two sons ; the one professing disobedience, but ultimately acting in obedience ; the second professing obedience, but failing therein. Having uttered His parable, He asked them which of the twain did the will of His Father, and they immediately replied, " The first," and so uttered the word of their own condemnation. He thus brought against them a charge that they had been professing to do the will of God, while their deeds contradicted their profession. Publicans and harlots who had openly rebelled but who repented, passed into the Kingdom of God from which these rulers were excluded. Moreover the sin of these self-satisfied religionists had been added to by the fact that when they saw the publicans and harlots believing, and changing their lives, they still refused to repent.

B. *As to Motives*

The next parable was that of the husband-men who failed to yield to the owner of the vineyard the fruits which were his due, ill-treating his servants, and finally slaying the son, that they might obtain the inheritance for themselves. Having uttered the parable, the King asked them what the lord of the vineyard would do in such a case as that ; and again they immediately answered that he would miserably destroy such men, and let his vineyard to other husbandmen, who would render him the fruit. Thus they not only found a verdict against themselves, but passed sentence ; which the King immediately applied so directly that " they perceived that He spake of them." This parable constituted the most terrific indictment of the nation which these men represented. They had received the high privilege of great responsibility, and had prostituted their opportunity to the serving of their own selfish ends, and were at the moment within a few days of the culmination of their iniquity in the casting out and murder of the Son. Solemnly therefore, and with such emphasis that they could not mistake His meaning, He pronounced upon them the sentence that the Kingdom of God was taken from them, and given to a nation bringing forth the fruits thereof.

γ. *As to their Rejection of the Kingdom*

The two previous parables had contained the history of the Hebrew nation up to the slaying of the Son. The one which the King now uttered was prophetic, and presented the sin of these people in the light of the day of grace which would dawn as the result of His work on the Cross. The king first sent his messengers to call them that were bidden. That first call described the activity of His own ministry. They refused to come.

Then a second appeal would be made, and that second call was descriptive of the mission of the Holy Spirit through the apostles. Of this they would make light. Each would go to the material interest of the moment, his farm, his merchandise ; and the only attention they would pay to the messengers would be that of persecuting and killing them. Then the King's armies would come, and the city be destroyed. Within forty years of the crucifixion of Jesus this was literally fulfilled.

Beyond that, a new invitation would be issued. The King's messengers would be sent to the partings of the highways to call the hitherto unbidden ones, and so the table would be furnished with guests. The Jewish nation as a nation, not only rejected Jesus, they also refused the ministry of the Holy Spirit through the apostles.

The illustration of the man without a wedding-garment abides as a solemn warning to all those accepting the invitation to the feast, that they can only remain as they conform to the requirements of the King.

3. *The public Unmasking of the Rulers*

The enemies of the King now adopted a new method of attack which He made the occasion of their unmasking. They endeavoured to entangle Him in His talk, and three such attempts were made, first by a coalition of Pharisees and Herodians; secondly by the Sadducees; and thirdly by the Pharisees. The attack was maliciously clever and subtle, beyond anything which they had attempted before; but the unutterable folly of it was revealed, as in each case He answered in words of such wisdom as to finally silence them.

a. *Pharisees and Herodians. Political*

A coalition of Pharisees and Herodians who were entirely opposed in their political convictions, suggested a seeming political question.

The answer of the King was first that of stern denunciation as He called them hypocrites. He then called upon them to produce a coin, which He made an illustration of principle. That principle was two-fold. Men who share the privileges of government must contribute to the support of government. Relation to earthly government must be conditioned by responsibility to God. Thus He unmasked their wickedness and hypocrisy, and revealed the unutterable folly of their question.

β. Sadducees. Doctrinal

The Sadducees submitted to Him a problem involving their disbelief in the immortality of the spirit of man. Ostensibly it was a question as to relationships in resurrection, but it was asked by men who said there is no resurrection. It was on the face of it a flippant question, intended to ridicule the idea of a life beyond.

Again the King's answer was first a word of denunciation, in which He declared that these men were ignorant of their own Scriptures, and of the power of God. This He illustrated by reference to the Scriptures, in which God is recorded as having declared Himself to be the God of Abraham, the God of Isaac, and the God of Jacob. He referred to the declaration made to Moses, which was made long after these men were dead; and He then declared that God is not the God of the dead, but of the living. This answer revealed the fact that the conditions of the spiritual world cannot be measured by material conditions; while at the same time it affirmed the immortality of man.

The effect produced upon the multitudes was that they were astonished at His teaching.

γ. *Pharisees. Moral*

The problem suggested by the lawyer on behalf of the Pharisees was one touching morality, and the relative values of the words of the law. The question was framed with the intention of compelling Christ to magnify some one requirement of the law, and thus to minimise some of the other parts thereof. To this inquiry He replied without any word of denunciation, and His reply teaches that the greatest words of the law are those which include all the rest.

261

4. *The King's final Question. Concerning the Messiah*

Having thus silenced all His questioners, addressing Himself to the Pharisees, the King asked them what view they held concerning the Sonship of Messiah. Their reply was immediate and accurate, that He would be the Son of David.

He then suggested a problem to them. How did they account for it that David, in speaking of Messiah, should call Him Lord; how could He be at once David's Lord, and David's Son? They were entirely discomfited, and unable to reply to Him. Thus He revealed their ignorance of the mysteries of their own writings, and history; and at the same time brought them face to face with a problem in the solution of which is found also the key to the mystery of His own being.

iii. THE DOOM AND SENTENCE

This chapter is one of the most solemn and awful in the whole of the inspired volume. It records the last words of Jesus to the crowds. He summed up, He found His verdict, He pronounced sentence. It is awe-inspiring in its majesty, and terrible in its resistless force. With unwavering persistence and unfailing accuracy He revealed the true condition of the leaders of the people, their occupation with externalities and pettiness, and their neglect of inward facts and weightier matters. Here indeed, if ever, we have thoughts that breathe, and words that burn. One can almost feel the withering force of His strong and mighty indignation; indignation directed, not against the people, but against their false guides; and yet through all there is the consciousness of His wounded heart, for every woe is a wail, and the ultimate sentence becomes the cry of a mother over her lost child.

The chapter falls into three parts; the

King's introductory words to the multitudes and to the disciples; the uttering of the final woes; and the pronouncing of the final sentence.

a. INTRODUCTORY WORDS TO MULTITUDES AND DISCIPLES

In these brief and yet remarkable sentences the King contrasted false and true authority.

1. *False Authority. Scribes and Pharisees*

Directly referring to the scribes and the Pharisees He recognised the responsibility of their position as He declared that they sat on Moses' seat, and in so far as they occupied that position, He charged the multitudes that they were to obey them.

Then He revealed the failure of these men as He further charged the multitudes not to imitate them. Their failure had been personal, in that they had not lived according to the Mosaic teaching of which they had been the messengers. Their failure was relative, in that they had bound heavy burdens, and laid them on men's shoulders, an undoubted reference to the superimposition of tradition upon law, while yet they had entirely refused to help men to carry them. Finally He denounced the failure of their motive, as with fine and biting sarcasm He described them as acting to be seen of men, as loving the chief places at feasts and in synagogues, and salutations in the market-places.

2. *True authority. The new Scribes.*

Addressing Himself now evidently to His own disciples who were to be the new scribes, that is, the new interpreters of the moral order, He revealed to them what their responsibility would be. They were not to be called teachers, they were to recognise no human authority, neither were they to attempt to exercise authority in their own rights. They must recognise their relationship to their brethren, in their relationship to their Father, under the mastery of the Christ.

The law of their service was to be that

of greatness through service, and exaltation through humility.

b. THE FINAL WOES

Then turning back again to the false rulers, the scribes and the Pharisees, He uttered His seven woes, and no words more searching, more terrible ever fell from His lips. They fall into three groups; the first consisting of three woes revealing the failure of these men in relation to the Kingdom; the second consisting of three woes revealing their failure in personal life; and the last consisting of one final woe revealing their failure in relation to the King.

1. *The first Three. Relation to the Kingdom*

The first woe was pronounced upon the rulers for their opposition to the Kingdom. Through their action the door was shut against men. They would not enter in themselves, neither suffer others so to do.

The second woe was against their imitation of the Kingdom. Their action had been characterised by zeal, but it was zeal to proselytise to their own conceptions, and the result was that in the cases of those with whom they succeeded, they became doubly evil.

The third woe was against their perversion of the true order, in that they had lost their true sense of values, and made the gold of the temple more important than the temple itself; and the gift of greater sanctity than the altar.

2. *The second Three. Personal*

The fourth woe condemned their personal failure in ceremonial matters. They had concentrated attention upon the trifling, to the neglect of the essential.

The fifth woe condemned their personal moral failure. They had been punctilious about external cleanness, while they were inwardly corrupt.

The sixth woe denounced their spiritual failure. They had maintained an outward appearance of beauty, while they were dead and unclean.

3. *The final One. Relation to the King.*

The seventh woe was the most terrible of all as it denounced these men for their failure to realise the authority of the King, and their persistent opposition thereto. He first reminded them that they were the children of the slayers of His messengers, notwithstanding the fact that they had built sepulchres to the prophets, and garnished the tombs of the righteous, and declared that they would have had no part in the sins of their fathers.

In a sentence full of appalling revelation of their continuity in iniquity, He declared them to be the heirs of their fathers' wickedness as He said, " Fill ye up then the measure of your fathers." Then in the most terrible words He described their evil nature, and asked how they could escape the judgment of Gehenna. The last part of the woe was prophetic, as He declared that He would send prophets and wise men and scribes; and that they would kill and crucify and scourge and persecute them; and that in the doing of this, the long-continued wickedness of the persecution of the messengers of God from the slaying of Abel to the blood of Zachariah, would find culmination. All these things He finally announced would come upon that generation. How terribly this was fulfilled, the history of the generation following His crucifixion, and culminating in the destruction of Jerusalem, testifies.

c. THE SENTENCE

Having thus uttered the terrible woes against the false people, the King pronounced the doom of the city. The first impression which the words create is of the heart and compassion of the King.

He introduced the final sentence by the declaration of the fact that the persistent sin of the city had been in spite of His own desire to gather her children together, and cover them under the shelter of His wings.

Because of that persistence, the doom

was inevitable, and in one brief and awful word He declared it, " Behold, your house is left unto you desolate "; and proceeded to reveal the fact that the desolation would be caused by His withdrawal.

III. HIS PREDICTIONS TO HIS OWN

Having thus uttered the solemn words declaring the rejection of the Hebrew people, His mind evidently occupied with the processes of the Divine economy, the Lord uttered His predictions to His own.

These predictions are admittedly difficult of interpretation. It is well that this should be recognised, and that the student of them should remember that in the consideration of prophecy—using the word in its more restricted sense of foretelling,—it is not always easy to gain a true perspective of events. A simple illustration may help us. Standing at the end of one of our long straight streets illuminated by gas-lamps at night, those in the far distance seem to be close together. It is only as we come nearer that we see them fall into their proper proportion of distance. Herein is our difficulty in the study of all predictive prophecy.

The King's predictions were uttered in answer to the inquiry of His disciples, and the broad division of this section therefore is that of the disciples' inquiry, and the King's answer.

i. THE DISCIPLES' INQUIRY

As the King withdrew from the temple, His disciples drew His attention to the buildings thereof. It was a strange thing to do, for He had often been in the temple with them, and certainly was familiar with the buildings thereof. It can only be explained by the fact of the words of His sentence, in which He had said, " Behold, your house is left unto you desolate." Morison quotes the rabbis as having a saying, " He that never saw the temple of Herod never saw a fine building "; and it must have seemed incredible to the disciples that their Master could mean that so glorious a structure should be destroyed.

He immediately answered by the clearest possible declaration that this was what He did mean, as He said, " There shall not be left here one stone upon another, that shall not be thrown down."

Having said this, He went to the mount of Olives, and there His disciples came to Him privately, for more specific teaching on the great subjects suggested by His closing address to the crowds, and His prophecy concerning the temple. It is important that we should carefully observe their inquiry. The form in which they preferred it reveals two questions ; first, " When shall these things be ? " secondly, " What the sign of Thy coming, and of the consummation of the age ? " While there are two questions, it is evident that to their mind it was one inquiry ; that is to say, they supposed that all these things would transpire at one time. Now as a matter of fact, they asked three questions, although they did not understand that they were doing so. The method of the King's reply distinguishes between them, and we may thus tabulate them ; first, " When shall these things be ? " second, " What shall be the sign of Thy coming ? " third, " What shall be the sign of the end of the age ? "

ii. THE KING'S ANSWER

In reply to this involved inquiry, the King uttered first a word of warning, and then detailed predictions.

a. THE WARNING

The warning of the King is in itself a recognition of the difficulty of the subject about to be dealt with. The period of His absence would, in view of the fact that He had so distinctly declared He would come again, be the opportunity for men to come in His name, declaring themselves to be the Christ; and thus to lead many astray. Against that danger He warned His disciples in the words, "Take heed that no man lead you astray."

b. THE PREDICTIONS

In these predictions the subject is that of the King's coming and the consummation of the age. The subject is dealt with in a threefold application; first to Israel, secondly to the Church, and thirdly to the Nations. From the standpoint of a calendar merely, there is repetition, as for instance, when dealing with the application to Israel, the King dealt with matters in the immediate future, and those which are not even yet fulfilled; in application to the Church He dealt with her attitudes in the period between these two phases of application to Israel; and in application to the nations He dealt only with His coming in glory, and that national judgment preceding the establishment of the Kingdom on earth.

1. *As to Israel*

The King's prediction concerning Israel fell into three parts. The first briefly dealt with that which was immediate; the second had to do with the end; and the third consisted of teaching.

a. *The Immediate*

In answering their first question the King carefully distinguished between " these things," that is, the things of desolation and destruction, and "the end." The former He declared must come to pass, but the latter "is not yet." The wars and rumours of wars referred to those troubles culminating in the destruction of Jerusalem, but the declaration of the King was perfectly clear that the end was not yet.

β. *The End*

The paragraph beginning here has often been treated as applying to the destruction of Jerusalem, and there are senses in which such treatment may be justifiable. As we said by way of introduction to our study of this section, the question of perspective must never be lost sight of, and the fact that there are certain principles of the Divine activity, which are constantly being fulfilled in partial measure on the way to final fulfilment. Perhaps we may be helped to understand this by being reminded of the prophecy of Joel, in which the day of the Lord was declared to be present in the plague of locusts, imminent in the advance of an army, and yet future for ultimate fulfilment.

There can be no question however that the main value of this particular section is that of its future fulfilment, for whereas it may be, and undoubtedly is true that in some sense the Son of man came in the hour of Jerusalem's downfall, it is equally true that His coming was not the patent and definite advent which is now described.

Looking forward to the end we have first a description of the initial signs. These will consist of strife among the nations and the kingdoms of the world, and famines and earthquakes. That period of trouble will be one of persecution, apostasy, fidelity, and the proclamation of the good tidings of the Kingdom, as a testimony to the nations.

In view of that period the King uttered words of solemn warnings. The sign would be that of the fulfilment of the prophecy of Daniel, of the manifestation in the holy place of the abomination of desolation. It will be a period of terror and of travail,

away," thus indicating the certainty of the fulfilment of the Divine purpose; and also the words, "Of that day and hour knoweth no one, not even the angels of heaven, neither the Son, but the Father only," indicating the fact that it is not intended in the economy of God that there should be any fixing of this date according to human calendars.

Another aspect of the condition of affairs is revealed by the illustration taken from the days of Noah. Men in persistent unbelief will continue in all the exercises of material life until they are suddenly disturbed by the coming of the Son of man. That coming will be in judgment. Those taken are taken away in judgment, and those left are left for blessing in the establishment of the Kingdom.

The final words of teaching are words of warning, in which under the figure of a master of the house watching, men are charged to watch and to be ready.

2. *As to the Church*

We now come to that portion of the prophetic utterance in which the King made application of the fact of His coming to His Church. This He did by employing three parables, each having a particular value. The first is the parable of the household, revealing the communal responsibility of His people during the period of His absence. The second is the parable of the virgins, revealing their personal responsibility during the same period. The third is that of the parable of the talents, revealing their imperial responsibility, or their responsibility concerning His Kingdom interests.

a. *Parable of Household*

In the interval between the departure of the King and His return, His household is that of His Church, and the first responsibility of those who constitute the Church is mutual. Upon those who will be found faithful to the responsibility at

His coming, a blessing is pronounced. The inspiration of faithfulness is the expectation of His return ; and consequently where that expectation is weakened, and men say that the Lord tarrieth, they fail to fulfil their responsibility to each other. Such failure will be visited with severe punishment in the hour of His advent.

β. *Parable of Virgins*

The initial word "Then" gives us the time in which the Kingdom of heaven will be likened unto ten virgins. That Kingdom passes through many phases, but immediately prior to the advent of the King this will be its character. It is important that we carefully notice that the ten virgins are required in order to a correct apprehension of the Kingdom value of this parable. All are virgins, and all are professedly waiting for the coming of the bridegroom. Five are watching, and unready, and therefore are excluded from the marriage supper. We have no warrant for speaking of the foolish virgins as lost. The hour of crisis

288

arrives with the advent of the bridegroom, and those who have been unready are left to the darkness. This phase of the advent of the King is not His public manifestation when He shines as the lightning from the east to the west; but that in which He first gathers His own to be with Himself. Those excluded from the marriage supper will pass through the tribulation preceding His manifestation to Israel, and to the nations. In view of this the warning word is again uttered, " Watch therefore, for ye know not the day nor the hour "; but now in application to the Church.

γ. *Parable of Talents*

Here again, in order to right interpretation of the parable, we must remember that it concerns the servants of the King. He has not committed His goods to rebels, but to His own. To apply this parable to all men, is to suppose that the absent Lord has committed His stewardship to rebels as well as to subjects. No greater mistake could be made. During the period of His absence there will be those faithful to the trust, and those unfaithful. Again the crisis will come with the return of the Lord, and His reckoning with His servants. Those who have been faithful will be appointed to share with Him in authority over His Kingdom. Those who have been unfaithful will be cast into the outer darkness. The outer darkness refers to the darkness and anguish of the period of tribulation, in which there shall be weeping and gnashing of teeth ; that is, manifestations of grief and disappointment. Here again we have no warrant for applying these words in any other connection than that in which our Lord employed them. They are words characterised by awe-inspiring solemnity for the servants during the period of His absence. Neglect may issue in terrible loss. We may only be saved so as by fire.

3. *As to the Nations*

In this paragraph we have the King's outlook upon His advent in its application to the race. There are three matters of interest; first, the centre of order; secondly, the first exercise of authority; and thirdly, the uttering of sentences and verdicts.

a. The Centre of Order

The centre of the new order will be the Son of man, manifested in His glory, occupying the throne, and surrounded by His angels.

β. The first Exercise of Authority

Being thus manifested, all nations will be gathered before Him, and in their gathering, separated into two camps ; the sheep on His right hand, and the goats on His left.

γ. Sentences and Verdicts

The judgment now described is not that of the saints, nor is it that of the race,

considered as individuals. It is, as He so
distinctly declared, that of the nations as
such. There are three classes, those on
the right, sheep; those on the left, goats;
and, "these My brethren." The separation
between the nations depends upon their
attitude toward His brethren. The basis
of the King's dealings with the nations
will be that of their treatment of the
house of Israel, and that with special
reference to the period of tribulation immediately preceding His manifestation.
There are nations which will be admitted
to the inheritance of the Kingdom. They
are such as have received Him, as He
has been represented in His people Israel
during the period of their terrible suffering
and their proclamation of the Gospel of the
Kingdom. There are nations which will
be excluded from that inheritance, and
banished to the darkness and the age-
abiding fire prepared for the devil and his
angels. They are such as have not received Him during that same period of
Israel's suffering testimony.

His Passion

This final application needs an accurate appreciation of all the events which have been taken into account in these predictions of the King.

IV. HIS TRAVAIL AND TRIUMPH

In this final section of the Gospel according to Matthew we are brought into the presence of the most sacred and awe-inspiring matters. We come to these final hours and activities toward which everything has been moving, and it is well that we should recognise at once that the dignity and reticence of the record is suited to the vastness of the theme, and is an indication of the reverence with which it should ever be approached.

The section has three movements, the first dealing with preliminary matters; the second introducing us to the actual hours of travail; and the third giving an account of the glorious triumph.

i. PRELIMINARY MATTERS

The preliminary matters were those of the passover feast; and the record contains an account of the approach thereto, and the observance thereof.

a. THE APPROACH

The King now reverted to the theme of His coming suffering, and with great definiteness, both as to time, and as to the actual event which was imminent. He reminded them that after two days the passover was coming, and declared that "The Son of man is delivered up to be crucified."

Meanwhile the priests and elders were assembled in secret conclave, plotting how they might secure Him, in order to silence His voice, by putting Him to death. Thus in this brief paragraph there is a remarkable illustration of the out-working of Divine purpose through the wrath of man. Both the King and His enemies were moving within the circle of the Divine government; He, delighting in the will of God, and they, all unknowingly, and in spite of themselves, acting in order to the accomplishment of that will. None can escape the operation of the Divine government. These men perhaps thought

298

that they were instruments accomplishing the purpose of God, but how little did they understand in what sense this was true. How dense is the darkness into which men fall who turn the light that is in them to darkness.

PARENTHESIS

The paragraph which follows is necessary in order to prepare for the action of Judas. It is not placed by Matthew in strict chronological order. As we have seen, the King definitely declared to His disciples the hour of His crucifixion two days before the passover. In the Gospel of John (xii. 1), we are told that this anointing of Jesus by Mary occurred six days before the passover. Its placing here in immediate connection with the story of Judas serves a twofold purpose. The action of Mary in itself is a revelation of perhaps the most wonderful and touching expression of love the Saviour ever received, while the action of Judas was the most dastardly to which He was ever subjected. Mary's love is the brightest gleam, and Judas' treachery the darkest shade in these final hours. It is important moreover, that they should thus be closely connected, and that the one should have led directly to the other. Contact with Christ in the neighbourhood of the Cross always brings the true character to the light. The strong sympathetic love of Mary, and the instinct of greed which cursed Judas, are revealed at the same time.

The action of Mary according to the King's interpretation of it, was a revelation of the fact that she had in some measure apprehended the sorrows of His heart.

The criticism of the disciples was a revelation of how far they were away from Him in these days of His supreme sorrow.

His defence of Mary is full of beauty, and constitutes the only occasion when He suggested that a memorial should be granted to any one in this world.

The effect of His defence of Mary on Judas was that he immediately found his way to the chief priests, and made his bargain with them to deliver his Master to them for thirty pieces of silver. It should be remembered that this happened six days before the passover.

b. THE PASSOVER

In preparation for the observing of the feast the disciples sought to know the will of the King, and having learned it, made all necessary arrangements. We have no full description of the feast. Its observance is referred to in the words, " He was sitting at meat with the twelve disciples," and this leads at once to the chronicle of the solemn revealing He made to them concerning His betrayal. That revelation being made, and the solemn words having been uttered concerning the betrayal " Good were it for that man if he had not been born," Judas directly challenged the Lord as to whether He referred to him, and was immediately answered in the affirmative. Differences of opinions exist as to whether Judas remained to the institution of the new ordinance. Personally I believe that he did

301

not, but that at this moment of revelation, he withdrew from the company.

The King immediately instituted that simplest and sublimest of all ordinances, as He took bread and a cup, and gave them to His disciples as symbols of His work for them, and their fellowship with Him. Beyond this observance, they joined in a hymn. There can be little question that it was the great Hallel, constantly sung at the passover feast, consisting of Psalms one hundred and thirteen to one hundred and eighteen, in our Psalter.

Thus in these hours the old economy ended, and the new began. Jesus ate the passover feast with His own loyal subjects and Judas. Never in all the history of that great feast had it been so sublimely kept. It was the culmination of the old economy, and the attitude of its failure was revealed by the presence and the act of Judas. He was the true representative at that board of the nation which had rejected the Messiah. Before the new feast,—growing out of the old in the infinite grace of God, by that dark act of treachery symbolic of the nation's failure,—was instituted, Judas had gone out. Only loyal souls took that bread and wine of the new covenant, revealing for ever the character of those who should partake of the ordinance. Strikingly impressive is the fact that as the King took these symbols of His coming suffering, and handed them to His loyal followers, He gave thanks, and declared that they symbolised His ability to deal with sin.

ii. THE TRAVAIL

In the actual account of the travail of the King we have first, the occurrences in Gethsemane ; secondly, the trial scenes ; and finally, the Cross itself.

a. GETHSEMANE

It is impossible to come to this story of Gethsemane without realising the necessity for reverent recognition of our inability to follow the King beyond a certain distance. Here He passed into a darkness where we cannot accompany Him, and we can only reverently observe Him as He moved through the vestibule to the altar of dedication, and emerging therefrom, was arrested by His enemies.

1. *The Vestibule. Preparing the Disciples*

The final hour was at hand, and the King definitely declared that in that very night they would be offended in Him. The smiting of the Shepherd would issue in the scattering of the sheep. This how-

ever was not His final word. That had
reference to the sure morning which would
follow the night, as He declared that
after He was raised, He would go before
them into Galilee.

In this connection again Peter protested
that he would never be offended in Him,
and that he was prepared to die for Him,
the declaration being made in spite of the
King's repetition of what, according to John,
He had declared in the midst of the paschal
discourses, that before the cock crew, he
should have denied Him thrice. Peter
was not alone in this attitude, for all the
disciples joined him in what he said.

2. *The Altar. Alone*

In this paragraph we see the King culminating that constant devotion to the
will of God, which had been the master-
principle of all His service. It was the
hour of solemn dedication which expressed
itself in three exercises of submission.

He first excluded eight of the disciples,
and then to three of them told the secret

of His sorrow. Having done so, He passed to the lonely act of dedication, which expressed itself in a submission which magnificently triumphed over His shrinking, as the unutterable woes of the Cross gathered about His soul. From that act of dedication He returned to His disciples, to find them asleep. With gentleness He chided Peter.

Again He left them, and expressed His dedication in a new word of submission to the will of His Father. Returning for the second time, He found the disciples still sleeping, and did not disturb them.

For the third and final time He moved to the loneliness, and uttered the same words of dedication. Returning to the disciples He first bade them sleep on and take their rest. Some have treated this almost as a word of rebuke or irony. I do not so understand it. How long the quiet time lasted I cannot tell, but I think the lonely Sufferer watched while they slept, as they could not watch while He suffered.

Then, the very hour being at hand, He
called them. What a tragic and pathetic
commentary does this story contain on the
weakness and instability of the very best
love and loyalty which are merely human.
Peter was not the only one sure of himself. Every man among them shared the
confidence. Yet there was not one of
them equal to an hour's vigil with the
King. Loyalty is nothing to be proud
of. It is a gift, for "no man can say,
Jesus is Lord, but in the Holy Spirit."
When we are tempted to criticise these
men, it is well that we should remember
that none of us would have acted differently
in those pre-Pentecostal days.

3. *The Emergence. Arrest*

Having faced and conquered the most
terrible trial in loneliness, and having rebuked in gentle tones of remonstrance the
sleeping three, the King turned to face
His foes ; and there again He met a threefold pain ;—the kiss of the traitor, the
blundering zeal of Peter, and the approach

of the fickle priest-ridden crowd. Judas came, leading the foes of his Lord, and giving them the sign of the kiss. To him Jesus spoke words of the gentlest tone as He said, "Companion, do that for which thou art come." Yet surely the words scorched as the very fire of hell.

In blundering zeal Peter drew his sword, and was immediately rebuked by the King, as He declared that He was not going to death as the result of the triumph of His enemies, for were not more than twelve legions of angels at His disposal? He was going of His own free will, and in order to fulfil the scriptures. This He made more emphatic by His gentle rebuke of the multitudes, and His declaration that everything that was happening was in fulfilment of the scriptures of the prophets.

It was then, when His disciples saw Him not arrested merely, but Himself consenting thereto, that they all forsook Him and fled.

b. THE TRIAL

Neither in the annals of the historian, nor in the realm of fiction is anything to be found that can equal the degradation and depravity revealed in the trial of Jesus. Let us examine this section in four parts, in the first of which we see Him rejected of men, chosen of God; in the second, denied by His own, yet saving them; in the third we have the doom of the traitor; and in the fourth, the appearance of the King before Pilate.

1. *Rejected of Men.   Chosen of God*

Arrested, the Lord was at once taken to the house of the high priest. Other of the evangelists show that there was first a halt made at the house of Annas, but they immediately moved on to the house of Caiaphas, where the Sanhedrin was assembled. Into the court of that house Peter followed, and sat with the officers to see the end.

The proceedings in the house of Caiaphas were of the basest. First there was a futile search for such false witness against Him as should create the possibility of the death sentence. At last two came who declared that He had said, " I am able to destroy the temple of God, and to build it in three days." A baser misrepresentation of what He had actually said it is impossible to conceive. His reference had been to His own body, and to their destruction of it. While it is true that they did not understand that, their witness was entirely false, for what He had said was, " Destroy this temple, and in three days I will raise it up." Thus, even according to their own understanding, He had not suggested that He would destroy the temple, but that if they did, He was able to rebuild. To this false charge He made no answer ; and then the high priest, leaving it out of count, put Him, in legal form, upon His oath as to whether He were the Christ, the Son of God ? His reply was a direct and positive affirmative, emphasised by the proclamation of His second advent in power.

This was enough. He was charged with

blasphemy, and the Sanhedrin's verdict was that He was worthy of death. The finding of the verdict was followed by the heaping of indignities upon Him.

2. *Denied by His Own. Saving them*

Here Matthew inserts the story of Peter's denial. It was a threefold experience. In answer to the challenge of a maid, he denied by equivocation as he said, " I know not what thou sayest." In answer to the declaration of a second maid, he denied on oath; and in answer to the challenge of others, he denied with curses.

Immediately the third denial had passed his lips the cock crew. Matthew does not record the coincident look of the Lord, but emphasises the fact that he remembered his Master's words; and immediately there was an emotional return, as going out into the darkness of the night, he wept bitterly.

3. *The Doom of the Traitor*

The morning saw the technically legal, but essentially iniquitous, carrying into effect of the plot hatched in the night. The Sanhedrin bound Him, and led Him away, and delivered Him to Pilate.

When Judas saw that He was condemned, he was filled with the most terrible remorse, and hurrying into the presence of the Sanhedrin, made his futile protest. The picture of his agony is most terrible. The sorrows of Satan are very real and very awful. A glimpse of them is surely seen in this terror of Judas, of whom Jesus had said, " One of you is a devil." To imagine that the devil gains any satisfaction from the awful work of evil is to misunderstand the true nature of evil. His is the consciousness of consuming and unsatisfied desire, the perpetual and awful agony of thwarted designs. Let such as hope to gain advantage by the way of sin remember that Judas gained nothing, not even the thirty pieces of silver, for these he returned to the priests, and the clangour of them on the sanctuary floor sounds across the centuries as an awful warning against the unprofitableness of ungodliness. Yet is it not a suggestive fact that with that blood money they bought the field of the potter? The field of the potter is the place of marred and spoiled vessels, and it was bought by the blood money of the Son of God.

4. *The Appearance before Pilate*

In the early morning Jesus stood before the representative of Roman power, who immediately challenged Him, "Art Thou the King of the Jews?" and was as immediately answered, "Thou sayest," a form of positive affirmation. To the accusation of the priests He made no reply, either directly, or through Pilate.

Pilate stands out on this page as a warning against the policy of expediency. He was convinced of the innocence of Jesus; and his conscience, perhaps more acute that day than it had been for a long time, plainly revealed to him that his duty lay in the direction of releasing the prisoner. This was the reason for offering them the choice between Barabbas and Christ.

It was while they had that offer before them that the warning came to him from his wife. This is but an incident, and yet it is impossible to pass it over without being impressed by the fact that the only voice raised on behalf of Jesus during the process of the travesty of justice, was that of Pilate's wife.

In response to the appeal of the governor, and instructed by the priests, the multitudes asked for Barabbas. In vain Pilate endeavoured now to save Him. He had attempted to save his conscience and his position; but when the alternative was forced back upon himself, he clung to position, and so flung Christ and conscience away. It was a vain and foolish thing, that washing of his hands in water, and the declaration that he was innocent. When a man does wrong under protest, in order to secure himself, he sacrifices himself. Thousands of men have endeavoured to get rid of Christ without actually rejecting Him. It has never been done, nor can it, when once the soul has stood face to face with Him.

His Passion

The most terrible of all human cries was that of the Jewish multitude as they accepted the issue of their choice in the awful words, "His blood be on us, and on our children."

c. THE CROSS.   OUTSIDE THE CAMP

The passage containing the actual story of Calvary is one which in certain applications must be read without note or comment. As we consider Him, there is nothing for it but to bow the head in worship, and to cry,

> "Oh love of God, oh sin of man,
>   In this dread act your strength is tried ;
> And victory remains with love,
>   For He, our Lord, is crucified."

As we come to the Cross it is necessary however, that we should observe the two-fold fact revealed therein in Matthew's account. We see Him first by the hand of lawless men ; and secondly, by the determinate counsel of God ; crucified and slain.

1. *"By the Hand of lawless Men"*

Delivered to His enemies, He first passed through the appalling preliminary mockery. They robed Him in scarlet, crowned Him with thorns, placed in His hand a reed, and then offered Him the homage of their contempt.

Having done so, they disrobed Him, and the procession proceeded to Golgotha; one, Simon of Cyrene being impressed to carry the Cross.

At last Golgotha, the place of a skull! In some brutal sense of pity ere the actual crucifixion, they offered Him drugged wine to drink, which He refused. How beautiful it is that Matthew does not tell the story of the crucifixion. Between our verses thirty-four and thirty-five, it happened. The next word considers it as accomplished, and tells how lawless men cast lots for His garments, and watched Him; how they set up over His head the accusation intended to anger the Jews, and yet proclaiming the Divine truth. His companions were robbers, and there moved backwards and forwards in front of the Cross, men who mocked His claims, and laughed at His impotence, knowing not that this impotence was the outcome of His all-conquering might, which was operating in order to make possible their forgiveness.

2. *" By the determinate Counsel . . . of God "*

From that terrible revelation of the human attitude to the Cross we turn to the more mysterious and yet wonderful revelation of the Divine relation thereto. Surely in the darkness that overspread the land there was more than the manifestation of Divine disapproval of human sin. Was it not also a revelation and an activity of Divine tenderness toward the dying King?

Out of the midst of the darkness at last there came the cry of humanity, " Eli, Eli, lama sabachthani ? " It is too profound for human interpretation, and the very fact that from the lips of the King it was a question, should for evermore remind those who would investigate, of the unfathomable wonder of that supreme hour of sorrow.

At the time it was entirely misunderstood, as the action of those who heard, reveals.

Again the voice from the Cross was

uttered in the very moment when the Spirit departed; and the Divine answer to that cry of victory, and that yielding of the Spirit was the rending of the veil of the temple from the top to the bottom, the immediate quaking of the earth, and the tearing of the rocks, and the opening of tombs, out of which three days after, following His resurrection, those who had been dead, arose and appeared in the holy city.

That death resulted in immediate illumination to some around the Cross, for the centurion in charge of the soldiers, and they that were with him cried out, " Truly this was a Son of God."

The scene is full of suggestiveness. The persons gathered around the Cross arrest attention. There were soldiers of Rome, for the most part debased and brutalised men. There were chief priests, scribes, and elders, filled with malice and envy, mocking Him; yet even in their mockery uttering under the constraint of God, abiding truths, " He saved others ; Himself He cannot save." Thieves were the companions of His Cross and death, and they were divided then and for ever by their attitude toward Him. And yonder was a group of women watching all in the distance. That mixture was surely a prophecy. All sorts and conditions of men have been attracted by that Cross, and have been influenced by it according to the manner of their approach. Some have watched, some have mocked, some have been healed.

iii. THE TRIUMPH

This is the last page in the Gospel of the King, and it is radiant in glory. Three pictures are presented to us ; those of the King resting ; the King risen ; and the King reigning.

a. THE KING RESTING

In this brief paragraph we see the ministry of love, and the activity of hate.

1. *The Ministry of Love*

The ministry of love is manifested in Joseph of Arimathæa and the Maries. Man in his enmity against God, had done his worst when he lifted the King to the tree. After that, no rebellious hand touched Him. Joseph of Arimathæa, a rich man, and a disciple of Jesus, begged the body, and with tender solicitude prepared it for burial, and laid it in his own new tomb hewn in the rock. It is a significant fact that not one of His apostles helped in His burying. The two men who attended to this sacred service were this Joseph, and as John reveals in his Gospel, Nicodemus. Both of these had been secret disciples. How often it happens that timid shrinking souls seem to be strongest in the hours of greatest need. Two women watched this laying to rest of the sacred body of the King.

2. *The Activity of Hate*

The persistent opposition of the enemies of the King was manifested in their fear after that He was dead ; and in the method which they adopted to make impossible the realisation of that which they feared. They remembered that He had said He would rise again, and requested that the sepulchre should be made sure until after the third day. If it were not so inexpressibly sad as a revelation of hard-hearted unbelief, it would be ludicrous, this folly of attempting to guard the dead body of Jesus on the part of His enemies. Was the irony of Pilate conscious, one wonders, when he said, "Make it as sure as ye can"? They were afraid of the Nazarene, even though He were dead. It is ever thus. The men who most strenuously oppose have a weird consciousness of Him that cannot be shaken off. Surely He liveth.

b. THE KING RISEN

In this paragraph we have the story of the sequel to that already considered, for herein we have the reward of love, and the discomfiture of hate.

1. *The Reward of Love*

When, as the first gleams of the dawn were shining on the Eastern sky, the Maries came to see the sepulchre, they found it empty, and under the guardian care of an angel. Matthew's brief story of the coming of the angel, and the accompanying earthquake is inserted at this point in order to account for the presence of the angel. To them the angel declared that the Lord was risen. " He is not here . . . He is risen." That surely was the sweetest of all music. It was the declaration not merely of His resurrection, but of His coronation. His that all authority was given to Him both in heaven and in earth ; and as resourceful as He the risen One was in Himself, for He promised to be always with the messengers, even to the consummation of the age.

So ends the Gospel of the King. He came and declared the laws of the Kingdom, and revealed its beauty in His life, and its beneficence in His deeds. His own, according to the flesh, would have none of Him, and in unholy coalition with Gentile powers, uttered the verdict, "We will not have this Man to reign over us."

Yet the final note is not that of man's rejection of the King, but of God's exaltation of Him ; and we are gathered around the risen One, and cry no longer as the expression of a desire, Long live the King ; but as the proclamation of a certainty, For ever lives the King.

Printed by Hazell, Watson & Viney, Ld., London and Aylesbury.

A SELECTED LIST of WORKS IN THEOLOGICAL AND RELIGIOUS LITERATURE AND BIOGRAPHY PUBLISHED BY HODDER AND STOUGHTON ALPHABETICALLY ARRANGED

Hodder & Stoughton, Publishers, Warwick Sq., London, E.C.

THEOLOGICAL AND RELIGIOUS LITERATURE

BLACK (Rev. Prof. HUGH, M.A., D.D.)
HAPPINESS.   2/- net.
FRIENDSHIP   2/- net.
WORK.   2/- net.
THE PRACTICE OF SELF CULTURE.   2/- net.
COMFORT.   2/- net.
CULTURE AND RESTRAINT.   6/-
EDINBURGH SERMONS.   6/-
CHRIST'S SERVICE OF LOVE   6/-

BLACK (Rev. JAMES, M.A.)
THE PILGRIM SHIP.   6/-

BLAIKIE (Rev. Prof. W. G., D.D., LL.D.)
THE FIRST BOOK OF SAMUEL. 7/6
THE SECOND BOOK OF SAMUEL. 7/6
THE BOOK OF JOSHUA.   7/6
WILLIAM GARDEN BLAIKIE: AN AUTOBIOGRAPHY.
Edited, with an Introduction, by Norman L. Walker, D.D. With Portrait.   6/-

BLAKE (Rev. BUCHANAN, D.D.)
THE BOOK OF JOB AND THE PROBLEM OF HUMAN SUFFERING.
Part I.—The Text of the Book rendered in metre. Part II.—The Problem of the Book.   6/-

BONAR (Rev. A. A., D.D.)
HEAVENLY SPRINGS.
Leather, 2/6 net; cloth, 1/6 net.
WAYSIDE WELLS.   Leather, 2/6 net.
Cloth, 1/6 net.

BRACE (C. LORING)
GESTA CHRISTI: A HISTORY OF HUMANE PROGRESS UNDER CHRISTIANITY.   7/6

BROADUS (JOHN A., D.D.)
THE PREPARATION AND DELIVERY OF SERMONS.   10/6

BROUGHTON (LEN G., D.D.)
SALVATION AND THE OLD THEOLOGY.   2/6 net.
THE PRAYERS OF JESUS.   2/- net.
THE KINGDOM PARABLES AND THEIR TEACHING.   2/- net.

BROWN (GEORGE)
GEORGE BROWN, MISSIONARY AND EXPLORER.
Illustrated, 15/- net.

BRUCE (Rev. Prof. A. B., D.D.)
THE GALILEAN GOSPEL   3/6
THE PARABOLIC TEACHING OF CHRIST.   12/-
THE MIRACULOUS ELEMENT IN THE GOSPELS.   12/-

BURNS (Rev. JAMES, M.A.)
REVIVALS. THEIR LAWS AND LEADERS.   6/-

BURTON (Rev. HENRY, M.A.)
THE GOSPEL OF ST. LUKE.   7/6

CADBURY (RICHARD)
A BIOGRAPHY. By Helen Alexander.
Illustrated, 7/6 net.

CAIRNCROSS (Rev. T. S., B.D.)
THE STEPS OF THE PULPIT. 3/6

CAIRNS (Rev. D. S., M.A.)
CHRISTIANITY IN THE MODERN WORLD.   6/-

CAMPBELL (Rev. R. J., M.A.)
THE RESTORED INNOCENCE.   1/6

CARTER (Rev. HENRY)
THE CHURCH AND THE NEW AGE.   2/6 net.

CARUS-WILSON (Mrs. ASHLEY, B.A.)
CLEWS TO HOLY WRIT: or, The Chronological Scripture Cycle.   2/-
MISSIONARY CLEWS TO THE NEW TESTAMENT.   3/6
THE EXPANSION OF CHRISTENDOM. A STUDY IN RELIGIOUS HISTORY.   6/-
IRENE PETRIE. Missionary to Kashmir. New edition, 2/6 net.

CHADWICK (Right Rev. G. A., D.D.)
THE GOSPEL ACCORDING TO ST. MARK.   7/6
THE BOOK OF EXODUS.   7/6
AIDS TO BELIEF.   1/6

CHADWICK (Rev. SAMUEL)
HUMANITY AND GOD.   2/6 net.

Hodder & Stoughton, Publishers, Warwick Sq., London, E.C

THEOLOGICAL AND RELIGIOUS LITERATURE

CHAPMAN (Rev. J. WILBUR, D.D.)
THE PROBLEM OF THE WORK. 5/-

CHRISTIAN STUDY MANUALS.
Edited by the Rev. Prof. R. E. Welsh, M.A., D.D. 1/- net each.
RULING IDEAS OF OUR LORD. By the Right Rev. C. F. D'Arcy, D.D. Lord Bishop of Clogher.
RELIGIONS OF BIBLE LANDS. By Rev. Prof. D. S. Margoliouth, D.D., D.Litt.
THE EARLY CHURCH: ITS HISTORY AND LITERATURE. By Rev. Prof. James Orr, D.D.
PROTESTANT PRINCIPLES. By Rev. J. Monro Gibson, D.D.
THE MASTER AND HIS METHOD. By Rev. Principal E. Griffith Jones, B.A.
THE SCENE OF OUR LORD'S LIFE. By Rev. Prof. Waddy Moss, D.D.

CLERICAL LIBRARY. Complete in twelve volumes. Price 5/- each. Special Subscription Terms on Application.
(1) THREE HUNDRED OUTLINES OF SERMONS ON THE NEW TESTAMENT.
(2) OUTLINES OF SERMONS ON THE OLD TESTAMENT.
(3) PULPIT PRAYERS. By Eminent Preachers.
(4) OUTLINE SERMONS TO CHILDREN. With numerous Anecdotes.
(5) ANECDOTES ILLUSTRATIVE OF NEW TESTAMENT TEXTS.
(6) EXPOSITORY SERMONS AND OUTLINES ON THE OLD TESTAMENT.
(7) EXPOSITORY SERMONS ON THE NEW TESTAMENT.
(8) PLATFORM AIDS.
(9) NEW OUTLINES OF SERMONS ON THE NEW TESTAMENT. By Eminent Preachers. Hitherto unpublished.
(10) ANECDOTES ILLUSTRATIVE OF OLD TESTAMENT TEXTS.
(11) NEW OUTLINES OF SERMONS ON THE OLD TESTAMENT. By Eminent Preachers. Hitherto unpublished.
(12) OUTLINES OF SERMONS FOR SPECIAL OCCASIONS.

CLOW (Rev. Prof. W. M., B.D.)
THE CROSS IN CHRISTIAN EXPERIENCE. 6/-
THE DAY OF THE CROSS. 6/-
THE SECRET OF THE LORD. 6/-

COFFIN (Rev. HENRY SLOANE, D.D.)
SOCIAL ASPECTS OF THE CROSS. 2/6 net.

COX (SAMUEL, D.D.)
ECCLESIASTES: OR, THE PREACHER. 7/6

CROSBY (FANNY J.)
HER OWN STORY OF HER LIFE AND HYMNS. 3/6 net.

DALE (R. W., D.D., LL.D.)
THE EPISTLE TO THE EPHESIANS: ITS DOCTRINE AND ETHICS. 7/6
THE EPISTLE OF JAMES AND OTHER DISCOURSES. 6/-
THE LIVING CHRIST AND THE FOUR GOSPELS. 3/6
CHRISTIAN DOCTRINE. A SERIES OF DISCOURSES. 6/-
ESSAYS AND ADDRESSES. 6/-
CHRIST AND THE FUTURE LIFE. 1/- net.
IMPRESSIONS OF AUSTRALIA. 5/-
FELLOWSHIP WITH CHRIST. 3/6
LAWS OF CHRIST FOR COMMON LIFE. 3/6
NINE LECTURES ON PREACHING. 6/-
THE JEWISH TEMPLE AND THE CHRISTIAN CHURCH. 6/-
WEEK-DAY SERMONS. 3/6
THE TEN COMMANDMENTS. 5/-
THE LIFE OF R. W. DALE, LL.D., OF BIRMINGHAM. By his Son. A. W. W. Dale, M.A. With portrait. 6/-
A HISTORY OF ENGLISH CONGREGATIONALISM. Completed and edited by A. W. W. Dale, M.A. 12/- net.

DARLOW (Rev. T. H., M.A.)
VIA SACRA. 3/6
THE PRINT OF THE NAILS. 1/6

Hodder & Stoughton, Publishers, Warwick Sq., London, E.C.

THEOLOGICAL AND RELIGIOUS LITERATURE

DAVIES (Rev. E. O., B.Sc., Lond.)
THEOLOGICAL ENCYCLOPEDIA:
An Introduction to the Study of
Theology. 5/-

DAVISON (Rev. Principal W. T., M.A., D.D.)
THE INDWELLING SPIRIT. 6/-

DAWSON (Rev. W. J., D.D.)
THE DIVINE CHALLENGE
3/6 net.
ONE NIGHT IN BETHLEHEM.
1/6 net.

DEISSMANN (Prof. ADOLF, D.D.)
LIGHT FROM THE ANCIENT
EAST. With Illustrations. 16/- net.
ST. PAUL. Translated by Lionel R.
M. Strahan M.A. 5/- net.
THE PHILOLOGY OF THE GREEK
BIBLE. Its Present and Future.
Translated by Lionel R. M. Stra-
chan M.A. 3/- net.

DENNEY (Rev. Prof. JAMES, D.D.)
THE WAY EVERLASTING. 6/-
THE DEATH OF CHRIST. A new
and revised edition, containing "The
Atonement and the Modern Mind."
6/-
THE EPISTLES TO THE THESSA-
LONIANS. 7/6
THE SECOND EPISTLE TO THE
CORINTHIANS. 7/6
STUDIES IN THEOLOGY. 5/-
THE ATONEMENT AND THE
MODERN MIND. 2/6
JESUS AND THE GOSPEL. 10/6
THE CHURCH AND THE KING-
DOM. 1/- net.
GOSPEL QUESTIONS AND AN-
SWERS. Cloth, 1/- net.
THE LITERAL INTERPRETATION
OF THE SERMON ON THE
MOUNT. 1/- net.

DICKIE (Rev. W., D.D.)
THE CULTURE OF THE SPIRIT-
UAL LIFE. 6/-
LIFE'S IDEALS 3/6

DOBSCHUTZ (Prof. E. VON, D.D.)
THE ESCHATOLOGY OF THE
GOSPELS. 5/-

DODS (Rev. Principal MARCUS, D.D.)
THE LATER LETTERS OF PRIN-
CIPAL MARCUS DODS. Edited by
his Son. 6/-
THE EARLY LETTERS OF MAR-
CUS DODS, Edited by his Son. 6/-
WHY BE A CHRISTIAN? 1/- net.
THE VISIONS OF A PROPHET.
1/- net.
ISRAEL'S IRON AGE. 3/6
ERASMUS AND OTHER ESSAYS.
5/-
THE PRAYER THAT TEACHES
TO PRAY. 1/6 net.
MOHAMMED, BUDDHA, AND
CHRIST: 3/6
ISAAC, JACOB AND JOSEPH 3/6
THE PARABLES OF OUR LORD.
(Matthew.) 3/6
THE PARABLES OF OUR LORD.
Second Series. (Luke.) 3/6
AN INTRODUCTION TO THE
NEW TESTAMENT. 2/6
THE BOOK OF GENESIS. 7/6
ST. JOHN. Vol. I. 7/6
ST. JOHN. Vol. II. 7/6
THE FIRST EPISTLE TO THE
CORINTHIANS. 7/6
FOOTSTEPS IN THE PATH OF
LIFE. Meditations and Prayers.
3/6 net.
CHRIST AND MAN: SERMONS. 6/-
THE LITERAL INTERPRETATION
OF THE SERMON ON THE
MOUNT. 1/- net.

DRIVER (Rev. Canon S. R., D.D.)
THE BOOK OF JEREMIAH. 6/- net.

**DRIVER (Rev. Canon S. R., D.D.) and
KIRKPATRICK (Rev. A. F., D.D.)**
THE HIGHER CRITICISM. New
and revised edition. 1/- net.

DRUMMOND (Prof. HENRY, F.R.S.E.)
NATURAL LAW IN THE SPIRIT-
UAL WORLD. 3/6
Popular edition. 6d.
THE ASCENT OF MAN. 3/6 net.
Popular edition. 6d.
THE CITY WITHOUT A CHURCH.
Cloth, gilt edges. 2/6
White covers, 1/-
THE CHANGED LIFE.
White covers, 1/-

Hodder & Stoughton, Publishers, Warwick Sq., London, E.C.

DRUMMOND (Prof. HENRY).—contd.

PAX VOBISCUM. White

THE GREATEST THING IN THE WORLD. Cloth, gilt edges, 2/6
White covers, 1/-

THE PROGRAMME OF CHRIST-IANITY. Cloth, gilt edges, 2/6
White covers, 1/-

TROPICAL AFRICA.
With Map and Illustrations, 3/6

BAXTER'S SECOND INNINGS.
Popular edition, 6d.; cloth, 1/6

THE IDEAL LIFE, AND OTHER UNPUBLISHED ADDRESSES. 6/-

THE WILL OF GOD.
White covers, 1/- net.

THINGS UNSEEN.
White covers, 1/- net.

THE GOLDEN BOOK OF HENRY DRUMMOND.
Cloth, 1/6 net; leather, 2/6 net.

THE GREATEST THING IN THE WORLD. A new and decorative edition. 1/6 net.

THE LIFE OF HENRY DRUM-MOND, F.R.S.E. By George Adam Smith, D.D., LL.D. With portrait.
Cloth, 3/6

DRUMMOND (ROBERT J., D.D.)

FAITH'S CERTAINTIES. 5/-

EDWARDS (THOMAS CHARLES, D.D.)

A COMMENTARY ON THE FIRST EPISTLE TO THE CORINTHIANS. 10/6

THE EPISTLE TO THE HEBREWS. 7/6

THE EXPOSITOR'S BIBLE.

Edited by the Rev. Sir W. Robertson Nicoll LL.D.
Series I. to VII., six vols. each, 24/- net each set; Series VIII., seven vols., 28/- net; single vols. 7/6 each

FIRST SERIES.

COLOSSIANS AND PHILEMON.
By the Rev. Alexander Maclaren, D.D., D.Litt.

THE GOSPEL ACCORDING TO ST. MARK. By the Right Rev. G. A. Chadwick, D.D.

THE BOOK OF GENESIS. By the Rev. Principal Marcus Dods. D.D.

THE FIRST BOOK OF SAMUEL.
By the Rev. Prof. W. G. Blaikie, D.D. LL.D.

THE SECOND BOOK OF SAMUEL.
By the same Author.

THE EPISTLE TO THE HEBREWS.
By the Rev. Principal T. C. Ed-wards, D.D.

EXPOSITOR'S BIBLE.—contd.

SECOND SERIES.

THE EPISTLE TO THE GALA-TIANS. By the Rev. Prof. G. G. Findlay, D.D.

THE PASTORAL EPISTLES. By the Rev. A. Plummer, D.D.

THE BOOK OF ISAIAH, i.—xxxix.
Vol. I. By the Rev. Principal George Adam Smith, D.D., LL.D.

THE BOOK OF REVELATION. By Prof. W. Milligan, D.D.

THE FIRST EPISTLE TO THE CORINTHIANS. By the Rev. Principal Marcus Dods, D.D.

THE EPISTLES OF ST. JOHN. By the Most Rev. W. Alexander, D.D., D.C.L.

THIRD SERIES.

JUDGES AND RUTH. By the Rev. R. A. Watson, D.D.

THE PROPHECIES OF JEREMIAH.
By the Rev. C. J. Ball, M.A.

THE BOOK OF ISAIAH.
Chaps. xl. to lxvi. Vol. II. By the Rev. Principal George Adam Smith, D.D., LL.D.

THE GOSPEL OF ST. MATTHEW.
By the Rev. J. Monro Gibson, D.D.

THE BOOK OF EXODUS. By the Right Rev. G. A. Chadwick, D.D.

THE GOSPEL OF ST. LUKE. By the Rev. H. Burton, M.A.

FOURTH SERIES.

ECCLESIASTES OR THE PREA-CHER. By the Rev. Samuel Cox, D.D.

THE EPISTLES OF ST. JAMES AND ST. JUDE. By the Rev. Alfred Plummer, D.D.

THE BOOK OF LEVITICUS. By the Rev. S. H. Kellogg, D.D.

THE BOOK OF PROVERBS. By the Rev. R. F. Horton, D.D.

THE ACTS OF THE APOSTLES.
Vol. I. By the Rev. Professor G. T. Stokes, D.D.

THE GOSPEL OF ST. JOHN.
Vol. I. By the Rev. Principal Marcus Dods, D.D.

FIFTH SERIES.

THE EPISTLES TO THE THESSA-LONIANS. By the Rev. Professor James Denney, D.D.

THE GOSPEL OF ST. JOHN. Vol. II. By the Rev. Principal Marcus Dods, D.D.

Hodder & Stoughton, Publishers, Warwick Sq., London, E.C.

EXPOSITOR'S BIBLE.—contd.

THE BOOK OF PSALMS. Vol. I.
By the Rev. Alexander Maclaren,
D.D., D.Litt.

THE ACTS OF THE APOSTLES.
Vol. II. By the Rev. Professor
G. T. Stokes, D.D.

THE BOOK OF JOB. By the Rev.
R. A. Watson, D.D.

THE EPISTLE TO THE EPHES-
IANS. By the Rev. Professor
G. G. Findlay, D.D.

SIXTH SERIES.

THE EPISTLE TO THE PHILIP-
PIANS. By the Rev. Principal
Rainy, D.D.

THE FIRST BOOK OF KINGS. By
the Very Rev. F. W. Farrar, F.R.S.,
Dean of Canterbury.

THE BOOK OF JOSHUA. By the
Rev Professor W. G. Blaikie, D.D.,
LL.D.

EZRA NEHEMIAH. AND ESTHER.
By the Rev. Professor W. F.
Adeney, M.A.

THE BOOK OF PSALMS. Vol. II.
By the Rev. Alexander Maclaren,
D.D., D.Litt.

THE EPISTLES OF ST. PETER.
By the Rev. Professor J. Rawson
Lumby, D.D.

SEVENTH SERIES.

THE EPISTLE TO THE ROMANS.
By the Right Rev. Handley C. G.
Moule, M.A., D.D., Lord Bishop of
Durham.

THE SECOND BOOK OF KINGS.
By the Very Rev. F. W. Farrar,
F.R.S., Dean of Canterbury.

THE SECOND EPISTLE TO THE
CORINTHIANS. By the Rev. Professor James Denney, D.D.

THE BOOKS OF CHRONICLES. By
the Rev. Professor W. H. Bennett,
D.D. D.Litt.

THE BOOK OF NUMBERS. By
the Rev. R. A. Watson, D.D.

THE BOOK OF PSALMS. Vol. III.
By the Rev. Alex. Maclaren, D.D.,
D.Litt.

EIGHTH SERIES.

THE BOOK OF DANIEL. By the
Very Rev. F. W. Farrar, F.R.S.,
Dean of Canterbury.

THE BOOK OF JEREMIAH.
Chaps. xxi.-lii. By the Rev. Professor Andrew Harper, B.D.

THE BOOK OF DEUTERONOMY.
By the Rev. Prof. Andrew Harper,
B.D.

EXPOSITOR'S BIBLE.—contd.

THE SONG OF SOLOMON AND
THE LAMENTATIONS OF JERE-
MIAH. By the Rev. Professor W.
F Adeney M.A.

THE BOOK OF EZEKIEL. By the
Rev. Professor John Skinner, M.A.

THE BOOKS OF THE TWELVE
PROPHETS. By the Rev. Principal
George Adam Smith, D.D., LL.D.
In Two Volumes.

COMPLETE INDEX TO THE EX-
POSITOR'S BIBLE. By S. G.
Ayres, B.D.   7/6

EXPOSITOR'S DICTIONARY OF TEXTS

Complete in two Volumes. Containing
Outlines, Expositions, and Illustra-
tions of Bible Texts, and full refer-
ence to the best homiletical literature
Edited by Sir W. Robertson Nicoll,
M.A., LL.D., and Jane T. Stoddart,
with the co-operation of the Rev.
James Moffatt, D.D.

Vol. I.—GENESIS TO ST. MARK.

Vol. II.—THE GOSPEL OF ST.
LUKE TO THE REVELATION.

Over 1,000 pages in each Volume.
Price 25/- net each Volume.

EXPOSITOR'S GREEK TESTAMENT.

Edited by the Rev. Sir W. Robertson
Nicoll, LL.D.

Complete in Five Volumes. Price to
Subscribers, £3 15s. net the set of
five volumes. Single volumes, price
28/-; any two volumes, 30/- net.

VOLUME I.

THE SYNOPTIC GOSPELS. By the
Rev. Prof. A. B. Bruce, D.D.

GOSPEL OF ST. JOHN. By the
Rev. Principal Marcus Dods, D.D.

VOLUME II.

ACTS OF THE APOSTLES. By the
Rev. Prof. R. J. Knowling, D.D.

ROMANS. By the Rev. Prof. James
Denney, D.D.

FIRST CORINTHIANS. By the Rev.
Prof. G. G. Findlay, B.A., D.D.

VOLUME III.

SECOND CORINTHIANS. By the
Very Rev. Dean Bernard, D.D.

GALATIANS. By the Rev. Frederic
Rendall, M.A.

EPHESIANS. By the Rev. Principal
Salmond, D.D.

PHILIPPIANS. By the Rev. H. A.
A. Kennedy, D.Sc.

COLOSSIANS. By Professor A. S.
Peake, D.D.

Hodder & Stoughton, Publishers, Warwick Sq., London, E.C.

THEOLOGICAL AND RELIGIOUS LITERATURE

EXPOSITOR'S GREEK TESTA-MENT.—contd.

VOLUME IV.

I. and II. THESSALONIANS. By the Rev. James Moffatt, D.D.

I. and II. Timothy. By the Rev. Professor Newport J. D. White, D.D.

TITUS. By the same author.

PHILEMON. By the Rev. W. O. E. Oesterley, M.A., D.D.

JAMES. By the Rev. W. O. E. Oesterley, M.A., D.D.

HEBREWS. By the Rev. Principal Marcus Dods, D.D.

VOLUME V.

I. PETER. By J. H. A. Hart, M.A.

II. PETER. By the Rev. R. H. Strachan. M.A.

JOHN. By the Rev. Prof. David Smith, M.A., D.D.

JUDE. By the Rev. J. B. Mayor, Lit.D.

REVELATION. By the Rev. James Moffatt, D.D.

FAIRBAIRN (Rev. A. M., M.A., D.D., LL.D.)

STUDIES IN THE LIFE OF CHRIST. 9/-

THE CITY OF GOD. 7/6

THE PLACE OF CHRIST IN MODERN THEOLOGY. 12/-

RELIGION IN HISTORY AND IN MODERN LIFE. 3/6

CATHOLICISM: ROMAN AND ANGLICAN. 7/6

THE PHILOSOPHY OF THE CHRISTIAN RELIGION. 12/-

STUDIES IN RELIGION AND THEOLOGY. 12/- net.

FARRAR (The Very Rev. F. W., D.D.)

THE BOOK OF DANIEL 7/6

THE FIRST BOOK OF KINGS. 7/6

THE SECOND BOOK OF KINGS 7/6

FAUSSET (The Rev. Canon A. R., D.D.)

THE CRITICAL AND EXPOSITORY BIBLE CYCLOPÆDIA.
Illustrated, 3/6 net.

FENWICK (MALCOLM C.)

WITH THE CHURCH OF CHRIST IN COREA. An autobiographical Missionary Record. 3/6

FINDLAY (Rev. Prof. G. G., B.A., D.D.)

THE EPISTLE TO THE EPHES-IANS. 7/6

THE EPISTLE TO THE GALA-TIANS. 7/6

FELLOWSHIP IN THE LIFE ETERNAL. 10/6

FISHER (Professor GEORGE P., D.D., LL.D.)

THE HISTORY OF THE CHURCH. 12/-

THE GROUNDS OF THEISTIC AND CHRISTIAN BELIEF. 10/6

THE REFORMATION. New and revised edition. 10/6 net.

FOREIGN BIBLICAL LIBRARY

Edited by the Rev. Sir W. Robertson Nicoll, M.A., LL.D. Ten Volumes. 7/6 each.

(1) STILL HOURS. By Richard Rothe.

(2) BIBLICAL COMMENTARY ON THE BOOK OF PSALMS. By Prof. Franz Delitzsch. In 3 vols.

(3) A MANUAL OF INTRODUCTION TO THE NEW TESTAMENT. By Bernhard Weiss. In 2 vols.

(4) CHURCH HISTORY. By Pro-fessor Kurtz. In 3 vols.

(5) SELECTED SERMONS OF SCHLEIERMACHER. Translated by Mary F. Wilson.

FORSYTH (Rev. Principal PETER TAYLOR, D.D.)

CHRIST ON PARNASSUS. Lectures on Art, Ethic and Theology. 10/6 net.

RELIGION AND RECENT ART. With Illustrations by Holman-Hunt, Burne-Jones, and Rossetti. Revised and enlarged edition. 10/6 net.

THE HOLY FATHER AND THE LIVING CHRIST. 1/- net.

CHRISTIAN PERFECTION. 1/- net.

RELIGION IN RECENT ART. Illustrated, 10/- net.

POSITIVE PREACHING AND MODERN MIND. 5/- net.

SOCIALISM, THE CHURCH AND THE POOR. 1/- net.

MISSIONS IN STATE AND CHURCH. 6/-

THE CRUCIALITY OF THE CROSS. 5/-

THE PERSON AND PLACE OF JESUS CHRIST. 7/6 net.

THE WORK OF CHRIST. 5/-

Hodder & Stoughton, Publishers, Warwick Sq., London, E.C.

THEOLOGICAL AND RELIGIOUS LITERATURE

GAIRDNER (W. H. T., B.A.)
D. M. THORNTON: A Study in Missionary Ideals and Methods. With illustrations, 3/6 net.

GARVIE (Rev. Principal A. E., M.A., D.D.)
STUDIES IN PAUL'S GOSPELS.
7/6 net.
A GUIDE TO PREACHERS. 5/-
STUDIES IN THE INNER LIFE OF JESUS. 7/6 net.
THE CHRISTIAN CERTAINTY A-MID THE MODERN PERPLEXITY
7/6 net.

GIBSON (Rev. JOHN MONRO, M.A., D.D.)
THE UNITY AND SYMMETRY OF THE BIBLE. 1/- net.
THE GOSPEL OF ST. MATTHEW.
7/6
PROTESTANT PRINCIPLES.
1/- net.

GLOVER (Rev. ARCHIBALD, M.A.)
A THOUSAND MILES OF MIRACLE IN CHINA.
Illustrations and Map. 3/6

GODET (F., D.D.)
STUDIES ON THE NEW TESTA-MENT. 7/6
STUDIES ON THE OLD TESTA-MENT. 7/6
STUDIES ON ST. PAUL'S EPISTLES. 7/6

GORDON (CHARLES W.)
THE LIFE OF JAMES ROBERT-SON, D.D. Illustrated, 6/-

GORDON (A. J., D.D.)
THE TWOFOLD LIFE: or, Christ's Work for us and Christ's Work in us.
1/6 net; leather, 2/6 net.
IN CHRIST.
1/6 net; leather, 2/6 net.
ECCE VENIT.
Cloth, 2/- net; leather, 2/6 net.
THE HOLY SPIRIT IN MISSIONS.
3/6

GORDON (S. D.)
QUIET TALKS ABOUT THE WORLD'S SAVIOUR. 2/6 net.
QUIET TALKS ON PERSONAL PROBLEMS. 2/6 net.
QUIET TALKS WITH WORLD WINNERS. 2/6 net.
CALVARY. 1/- net.

GREENHOUGH (Rev. J. G., M.A.)
THE APOSTLES OF OUR LORD.
5/-
THE CROSS IN MODERN LIFE.
6/-
THE MIND OF CHRIST IN ST. PAUL 6/-

GRIFFITH-JONES (Rev. Principal E., B.A.)
THE ASCENT THROUGH CHRIST:
3/6
THE MASTER AND HIS METHOD.
1/- net.

HAERING (Professor)
THE HISTORY OF DOGMA. Translated by the Rev. Professor J. Dickie, D.D. 12/-

HENSON (Rev. Canon HENSLEY, D.D.)
THE ROAD TO UNITY. 1/- net.

HOLDEN (Rev. J. STUART, M.A.)
THE PRE-EMINENT LORD, and other Sermons. 3/6

HORTON (Rev. R. F., M.A., D.D.)
THE BOOK OF PROVERBS. 7/6

HOUSEHOLD LIBRARY OF EX-POSITION:
Nine volumes, 3/6 each.
THE LIFE OF DAVID AS RE-FLECTED IN HIS PSALMS. Rev. Alexander Maclaren, D.D., LL.D.
THE GALILEAN GOSPEL. Rev. Prof. A. B. Bruce, D.D., LL.D.
ISAAC, JACOB, AND JOSEPH. Rev. Principal Marcus Dods, D.D.
THE LAST SUPPER OF OUR LORD and His Words of Consola-tion to the Disciples. Rev. Princi-pal J. Marshall Lang, D.D.
THE SPEECHES OF THE HOLY APOSTLES. Rev. Donald Fraser, D.D.
THE LORD'S PRAYER. Rev. Chas. Stanford, D.D.
THE PARABLES OF OUR LORD. Rev. Principal Marcus Dods, D.D. Two volumes.
THE LAW OF THE TEN WORDS. Rev. Principal J. Oswald Dykes, D.D.

Hodder & Stoughton, Publishers, Warwick Sq., London, E.C.

THEOLOGICAL AND RELIGIOUS LITERATURE

HUGHES (HUGH PRICE)
THE LIFE OF HUGH PRICE HUGHES. By his Daughter.
Illustrated, 3/6 net.

HUTTON (Rev. JOHN, M.A.)
THE WINDS OF GOD. A Study of Nineteenth Century Thought in Relation to Faith. 2/6 net.

IVERACH (Rev. Prof. J., D.D.)
IS GOD KNOWABLE ? 3/6

JACKSON (Rev. GEORGE, B.A.)
THE TABLE-TALK OF JESUS. 3/6
FIRST THINGS FIRST. 3/6
A YOUNG MAN'S RELIGION. 3/6
THE TEACHING OF JESUS. 3/6
THE OLD METHODISM AND THE NEW. 1/-
THE FACT OF CONVERSION. 3/6

JONES (Rev. J. D., B.D.)
THE HOPE OF THE GOSPEL. 6/-

JONES (Rev. MAURICE, B.D.)
ST. PAUL THE ORATOR. 6/-

JOWETT (Rev. J. H., M.A., D.D.)
APOSTOLIC OPTIMISM. 6/-
FIRST AND SECOND EPISTLES OF PETER. 5/-
FROM STRENGTH TO STRENGTH 1/- net.

KELLOGG (Rev. Prof. S. H., D.D.)
THE BOOK OF LEVITICUS. 7/6

KELMAN (Rev. JOHN, D.D.)
EPHEMERA ETERNITATIS. 5/- net.

KENNEDY (Rev. H. A. A., M.A., D.Sc.)
ST. PAUL'S CONCEPTIONS OF THE LAST THINGS. 7/6 net.

KENT (Professor CHARLES FOSTER, Ph.D.)
THE STUDENTS' OLD TESTAMENT. Six vols., 12/- net each; special subscription terms for the six vols., £2 10s. net.
THE ORIGIN AND PERMANENT VALUE OF THE OLD TESTAMENT. 6/-
THE HISTORICAL BIBLE. Complete in six vols., 5/- net each.

KER (Rev. Prof. JOHN, D.D.)
LECTURES ON THE HISTORY OF PREACHING. Edited by the Rev. A. R. Macewen. A new edition. 6/-

KILPATRICK Rev. T. B., D.D.)
NEW TESTAMENT EVANGELISM. Part I.—Evangelism in the New Testament. Part II.—Evangelism in History. Part III.—Evangelism in the Modern Church. 5/-

KNIGHT (Rev. GEORGE H.)
THE MASTER'S QUESTIONS TO HIS DISCIPLES. 5/-
IN THE SECRET OF HIS PRESENCE. 3/6
IN THE CLOUDY AND DARK DAY 3/6

KNOWLING (Rev. Prof. R. J., D.D.)
THE TESTIMONY OF ST. PAUL TO CHRIST. A new and revised edition. 7/6

LAIDLAW (Rev. Prof. JOHN, D.D.)
THE MIRACLES OF OUR LORD. 7/6
STUDIES IN THE PARABLES, and other Sermons. 6/-

LATIMER (ROBERT SLOAN)
WITH CHRIST IN RUSSIA. 2/6 net

LINDSAY (Rev. Principal T. M., D.D.)
THE CHURCH AND THE MINISTRY IN THE EARLY CENTURIES. 10/6

LITTLE BOOKS ON RELIGION.
Edited by the Rev. Sir W. Robertson Nicoll, M.A., LL.D.
1/- net each.
FACTORS OF FAITH IN IMMORTALITY. Rev. Prof. James Denney, D.D.
LINDSAY ALEXANDER. E. T. Maclaren.
THE CHURCH AND THE KINGDOM. Rev. Prof. James Denney, D.D.
THE BOOK OF THE KINDLY LIGHT. J. S. Zelie, D.D.
ST. JOHN'S PORTRAIT OF CHRIST Rev. George Matheson, M.A., D.D.
THE LITERAL INTERPRETATION OF THE SERMON ON THE MOUNT. Rev. Marcus Dods, D.D., Rev. Prof. James Denney, D.D., and Rev. James Moffatt, D.D.

Hodder & Stoughton, Publishers, Warwick Sq., London, E.C.

THEOLOGICAL AND RELIGIOUS LITERATURE

LITTLE BOOKS ON RELIGION.—contd.

THE SECOND THINGS OF LIFE. Rev. James Moffatt, D.D.

PRAYER. Dora Greenwell, with Introduction by Rev. Principal P. T. Forsyth.

THE MYSTERY OF PAIN. James Hinton, with Introduction by R. H. Hutton.

DANTE. Dean Church.

THE UPPER ROOM. Rev. John Watson, D.D.

FROM STRENGTH TO STRENGTH. Rev. J. H. Jowett, M.A., D.D.

THE SEVEN DEADLY SINS. Rev. Prof. James Stalker, M.A., D.D.

CHRISTIAN PERFECTION. Rev. Principal P. T. Forsyth, D.D.

THE SEVEN WORDS FROM THE CROSS. Rev. W. Robertson Nicoll, M.A.. LL.D.

CHRIST AND THE FUTURE LIFE. Rev. R. W. Dale, D.D., LL.D.

THE FOUR TEMPERAMENTS. Rev. Alexander Whyte, D.D.

FOUR PSALMS. Rev. Principal G. A. SMITH, D.D., LL.D.

THE FOUR GOSPELS. Rev. R. H. Fisher, B.D.

WHY BE A CHRISTIAN? and other Addresses to Young Men. Rev Marcus Dods, D.D.

GOSPEL QUESTIONS AND ANSWERS. Rev. Prof. James Denney, D.D.

THE HOLY FATHER AND THE LIVING CHRIST. Rev. Principal P. T. Forsyth, D.D.

THE VISIONS OF A PROPHET. Rev. Principal Marcus Dods, D.D.

RESTORED INNOCENCE. Rev. R. J. Campbell, M.A.

THE UNITY AND SYMMETRY OF THE BIBLE. Rev. John Monro Gibson, M.A., D.D.

AIDS TO BELIEF. Rt. Rev. G. A. Chadwick, D.D.

THE SEVEN CARDINAL VIRTUES. Rev. Prof. James Stalker, D.D.

THE THREE THINGS THAT ABIDE : FAITH, HOPE, LOVE. Sir W. T. Gairdner, K.C.B.

LUMBY (Rev. J. RAWSON, D.D.)

THE EPISTLES OF ST. PETER.
7/6

MACALISTER (R. A. STEWART, M.A., F.S.A.)

BIBLE SIDE-LIGHTS FROM THE MOUND OF GEZER.
Illustrated, 5/-

MACFADYEN (Rev. Prof. J. E., D.D.)

THE INTERPRETER'S COMMENTARY ON THE EPISTLES.
Vol. I.—I. and II. Corinthians.   6/-

OLD TESTAMENT CRITICISM AND THE CHRISTIAN CHURCH.   6/-

AN INTRODUCTION TO THE OLD TESTAMENT.   6/-

THE PRAYERS OF THE BIBLE.
6/- net.

THE CITY WITH FOUNDATIONS.
5/-

MACKAY (Rev. J. H., M.A.)

RELIGIOUS THOUGHT IN HOLLAND DURING THE 19th CENTURY.   6/-

MACKAY (Rev. W. MACKINTOSH, B.D.)

BIBLE TYPES OF MODERN MEN.
6/-

MACKAY (A. M.)

MACKAY, A. M., Pioneer Missionary of the Church Missionary Society to Uganda. With etched portrait by Manesse   7/6

MACKINTOSH (Rev. Professor H. R., D.D.)

LIFE ON GOD'S PLAN and other SERMONS.   5/-

MACLAREN (Rev. ALEXANDER, D.D., D.Litt.)

THE PSALMS. Vol. I.   7/6
THE PSALMS. Vol. II.   7/6
THE PSALMS. Vol. III.   7/6
THE EPISTLE TO THE COLOSSIANS   7/6
THE LIFE OF DAVID AS REFLECTED IN HIS PSALMS.   3/6
THE VICTOR'S CROWNS, and other SERMONS.   5/-
TRIUMPHANT CERTAINTIES.   5/-

Hodder & Stoughton, Publishers, Warwick Sq., London, E.C.

THEOLOGICAL AND RELIGIOUS LITERATURE

MACLAREN (Rev. A.)—contd.

CHRIST IN THE HEART, and other SERMONS. 5/-
A YEAR'S MINISTRY. First Series. 5/-
A YEAR'S MINISTRY. Second Series. 5/-
SERMONS PREACHED IN MAN-CHESTER. First Series. 5/-
SERMONS PREACHED IN MAN-CHESTER. Second Series. 5/-
SERMONS PREACHED IN MAN-CHESTER. Third Series. 5/-
AFTER THE RESURRECTION. 5/-
LAST SHEAVES. 5/-
THE SECRET OF POWER, and other SERMONS. 5/-
WEEK-DAY EVENING ADDRESSES. Delivered in Manchester. 5/-
THE BEATITUDES. 5/-
THE WEARIED CHRIST. 5/-
THE GOD OF THE AMEN. 5/-
THE HOLY OF HOLIES. 5/-
CHRIST'S MUSTS. 5/-
PAUL'S PRAYERS. 5/-
THE UNCHANGING CHRIST. 5/-
LEAVES FROM THE TREE OF LIFE. 5/-
PULPIT PRAYERS. First Series. 7/6
PULPIT PRAYERS. Second Series. 7/6
EXPOSITIONS OF HOLY SCRIP-TURE. The First, Second, Third, and Fourth Series, of Six Volumes each, 24/- net each. The Fifth Series of Eight Volumes 32/- net the set. Single Volumes 7/6.

FIRST SERIES.

(1) THE BOOK OF GENESIS.
(2) THE BOOK OF ISAIAH. (Chapters i.-xlviii.)
(3) THE GOSPEL OF ST. MAT-THEW. Vol. I. (Chaps. i.-viii.)
(4) THE GOSPEL OF ST. MAT-THEW. Vol. II. (Chapters ix.-xvii.)
(5) THE GOSPEL OF ST. MAT-THEW. Vol. III. (Chapters xviii.-xxviii.)
(6) THE BOOK OF ISAIAH. (Chapters xlix.-lxvi.) and THE BOOK OF JEREMIAH.

MACLAREN (Rev. A.)—contd.

SECOND SERIES.

(1) THE GOSPEL OF ST. MARK Vol. I. (Chaps. i.-viii.)
(2) THE GOSPEL OF ST. MARK Vol. II. (Chaps. viii.-xvi.)
(3) EXODUS, LEVITICUS, NUM-BERS. 1 Volume.
(4) DEUTERONOMY, JOSHUA, JUDGES, RUTH, and 1st SAMUEL.
(5) 2nd SAMUEL, 1st KINGS, 2nd KINGS (to chap. vii.)
(6) THE ACTS OF THE APOSTLES Vol. I. (Chaps. i.-xiii.)

THIRD SERIES.

(1) THE ACTS OF THE APOSTLES Vol. II. (Chaps. xiii. to end.)
(2) THE GOSPEL OF ST. JOHN. Vol. I. (Chaps. i. to viii.)
(3) THE GOSPEL OF ST. JOHN. Vol. II. (Chaps. ix.-xiv.)
(4) THE GOSPEL OF ST. JOHN. Vol. III. (Chaps. xv.-xxi.)
(5) 2nd KINGS (from chap. viii.), CHRONICLES, EZRA and NE-HEMIAH.
(6) ESTHER, JOB, PROVERBS and ECCLESIASTES.

FOURTH SERIES.

(1) THE PSALMS. Vol. I. (Chapters i.-xlix.)
(2) THE PSALMS. Vol. II. (Chapters li.-cxlv.)
(3) EZEKIEL, DANIEL, and THE MINOR PROPHETS.
(4) ST. LUKE. Vol. I.
(5) ST. LUKE. Vol. II.
(6) THE EPISTLE TO THE RO-MANS.

FIFTH SERIES.

(1) I. and II. CORINTHIANS (to chapter v.)
(2) THE EPISTLE TO THE EPHE-SIANS.
(3) II. CORINTHIANS (completion), GALATIANS and PHILIPPIANS.
(4) COLOSSIANS to I. TIMOTHY.
(5) II. TIMOTHY, TITUS, PHILE-MON, HEBREWS.

Hodder & Stoughton, Publishers, Warwick Sq., London, E.C.

THEOLOGICAL AND RELIGIOUS LITERATURE

MACLAREN (Rev. A.)—contd.
(6) HEBREWS (completion) and ST. JAMES.
(7) I. and II. PETER, JOHN.
(8) II. and III. JOHN, JUDE and REVELATION.
BIBLE CLASS EXPOSITIONS.
Six volumes, 3/6 each.
(1) THE GOSPEL OF ST. MATTHEW. Vol. I.
(2) THE GOSPEL OF ST. MATTHEW. Vol. II.
(3) THE GOSPEL OF ST. MARK.
(4) THE GOSPEL OF ST. LUKE.
(5) THE GOSPEL OF ST. JOHN.
(6) THE ACTS OF THE APOSTLES

MACLEAN (Rev. NORMAN)
CAN THE WORLD BE WON FOR CHRIST?   2/6 net.

MACMILLAN (Rev. D., D.D.)
LIFE OF DR. GEORGE MATHESON.   2/6
THE ABERDEEN DOCTORS.   6/-

MARGOLIOUTH (Rev. Prof. D. S., M.A., D.D., D.Litt.)
LINES OF DEFENCE OF THE BIBLICAL REVELATION.   6/-
RELIGIONS OF BIBLE LANDS.   1/- net.

MARSTON (Rev. HERBERT J., M.A.,
REDEMPTION, RECONCILIATION, AND SANCTITY. Thoughts on the Christian Doctrine of Atonement. 3/6

MATHESON (Rev. GEORGE, D.D.)
SIDELIGHTS FROM PATMOS.   6/-
STUDIES OF THE PORTRAIT OF CHRIST. Two vols.   6/- each.
THE REPRESENTATIVE MEN OF THE BIBLE. First Series.   6/-
THE REPRESENTATIVE MEN OF THE BIBLE. Second Series—Ishmael to Daniel.   6/-
THE REPRESENTATIVE MEN OF THE NEW TESTAMENT.   6/-
REPRESENTATIVE WOMEN OF THE BIBLE.   6/-
RESTS BY THE RIVER: DEVOTIONAL MEDITATIONS.   6/-
ST. JOHN'S PORTRAIT OF CHRIST   1/- net.

MAUNDER (E. WALTER, F.R.A.S.)
THE ASTRONOMY OF THE BIBLE
Illustrated, 5/- net.

MILLER (Rev. ANDREW, M.A.,
THE PROBLEM OF THEOLOGY IN MODERN LIFE AND THOUGHT
5/-

MILLER (Rev. J. R., D.D.)
THE SILENT TIMES SERIES
3/6 each.
THE BEAUTY OF SELF-CONTROL.
THE GOLDEN GATE OF PRAYER.
FINDING THE WAY.
THE LESSON OF LOVE.
THE BLOSSOM OF THORNS.
THE UPPER CURRENTS.
THE MINISTRY OF COMFORT
STRENGTH AND BEAUTY.
THE JOY OF SERVICE
PERSONAL FRIENDSHIPS OF JESUS.
THINGS TO LIVE FOR.
MAKING THE MOST OF LIFE.
SECRETS OF A BEAUTIFUL LIFE
SILENT TIMES.
THE GATE BEAUTIFUL
THE EVERY-DAY OF LIFE.
WEEKDAY RELIGION.
A MESSAGE FOR THE DAY.
THE GARDEN OF THE HEART
THE WIDER LIFE.
THE GLORY OF THE COMMON LIFE.
THE BEST THINGS IN LIFE.

DR. MILLER'S ILLUSTRATED BOOKLETS
THE JOY OF THE LORD. 1/- net.
TO-DAY AND TO-MORROW.   1/-
BESIDE THE STILL WATERS. 1/-
UNTO THE HILLS.   1/-
IN PERFECT PEACE.   1/-
LOVING MY NEIGHBOUR.   1/-
THE SECRET OF GLADNESS. 1/-
THE FACE OF THE MASTER. 1/-
SUNSHINE WITHIN.   1/-
THE SMALL COIN OF LOVE. 1/-
GO FORWARD.   1/-
THE MASTER'S FRIENDSHIPS.
1/-
LEARNING TO LOVE.   1/- net.
THE SONG OF THE ANGELS. 1/-
THE GATES OF HEAVEN.   1/-

Hodder & Stoughton, Publishers, Warwick Sq., London, E.C.

THEOLOGICAL AND RELIGIOUS LITERATURE

MILLER (Rev. J. R.)—contd.

DEVOTIONAL HOURS WITH THE BIBLE. In eight volumes, 5/- each
Vol. I.—From the Creation to the Crossing of the Red Sea. (Ready.)
Vol. II.—From the Crossing of the Red Sea to the close of the life of David.
Vol. III.—The Gospel of St. Matthew
Vol. IV.—The Historical Books from Solomon to Malachi.
Vol. V.—The Life of Christ.

GOLDEN WEEK.
With cover printed in colour and gold, embossed. 6d.

GOLDEN MONTH.
With cover printed in colour and gold, embossed. 1/- net.

OUR NEW EDENS : AND OTHER MEDITATIONS. 1/- net.

THE STORY OF JOSEPH. 1/- net.

THE COMING OF JESUS CHRIST. 1/-

THE PATHOS OF DIVINE LOVE. 1/-

MORNING THOUGHTS AND EVENING THOUGHTS. 1/- each; or together in decorative box, 2/-

DR. MILLER'S SIXPENNY BOOKLETS
In new pictorial covers.

A GENTLE HEART.

THE BLESSING OF CHEERFULNESS.

SECRETS OF A HAPPY HOME LIFE.

WHAT IT IS TO BE A CHRISTIAN.

NEAR THE HEART OF CHRIST.

THE MASTER'S BLESSEDS

THE MASTER'S BENEDICTIONS

THE PROBLEM OF LIFE

MILLIGAN (Rev. Prof., D.D.)

THE BOOK OF REVELATION 7/6

MILMINE (GEORGINE)

MARY BAKER G. EDDY. The Story of her Life and the History of Christian Science.
Illustrated, 6/-

MORGAN (Rev. G. CAMPBELL, D.D.)

THE SPIRIT OF GOD. 3/6
THE CRISES OF CHRIST. 3/6 net.
CHRIST AND THE BIBLE. 1d.
THE PRACTICE OF PRAYER. 1/6
THE PARABLES OF THE KINGDOM. 2/6 net.
CHRISTIAN PRINCIPLES. 1/6 net.
THE MISSIONARY MANIFESTO. 2/- net.
THE BIBLE AND THE CROSS. 1/6 net.
THE STUDY AND TEACHING OF THE ENGLISH BIBLE.
Paper, 1/- net; cloth, 1/6 net.
THE ANALYSED BIBLE.
Cloth, 3/6 each vol.
(1) General Review of Genesis to Esther.
(2) General Review of Job to Malachi.
(4) The Gospel of St. John.
(5) The Book of Job.
(6) The Epistle of Paul the Apostle to the Romans.
(7) The Prophecy of Isaiah, Vol. I.
(8) The Prophecy of Isaiah, Vol. II.
(9) The Gospel of St. Matthew.
(10) The First and Second Epistles to the Corinthians.
THE MORNING MESSAGE. 2/-
MESSAGES OF THE BOOKS OF THE BIBLE. Vol. I. Genesis to Esther. Vol. II. Esther to Mark. Vol. III. The New Testament.
3/6 each.
THE TEACHING OF THE LESSON, 1912. A pocket commentary on the International Sunday School Lessons for 1912. 1/- net.
THE WESTMINSTER BOOKLETS.
With embossed covers printed in colours. Paper covers, 6d. each.
I.—To Die is Gain; II.—The Fulfilment of Life; III.—Enoch; IV.—The Purposes of the Incarnation; V.—But One Thing.
WESTMINSTER BIBLE STUDIES.
Seven booklets. Paper, 3d. each; Limp cloth, 6d. each.
The Acts of the Apostles.
The Epistle to the Romans.
The First Epistle to the Corinthians.
The Second Epistle to the Corinthians.
The Epistle to the Galatians.
The Epistle to the Ephesians.
The Epistle to the Philippians.

Hodder & Stoughton, Publishers, Warwick Sq., London, E.C.

THEOLOGICAL AND RELIGIOUS LITERATURE

MORISON (JAMES, D.D.)

A PRACTICAL COMMENTARY ON THE GOSPEL ACCORDING TO ST. MATTHEW. 14/-

A PRACTICAL COMMENTARY ON THE GOSPEL ACCORDING TO ST. MARK. 12/-

MORRISON (Rev. G. H., M.A.)

FLOOD TIDE. 5/-
SUN-RISE. 5/-
THE FOOTSTEPS OF THE FLOCK. 6/-
THE UNLIGHTED LUSTRE. 5/-
THE WINGS OF THE MORNING. 5/-
THE RETURN OF THE ANGELS. 5/-

MOTT (JOHN R., F.R.C.S.)

THE HOME MINISTRY AND MODERN MISSIONS. 3/6

THE FUTURE LEADERSHIP OF THE CHURCH. 3/6

MOULE (Rt. Rev. H. C. G., D.D.)

EPHESIAN STUDIES. 5/-
PHILIPPIAN STUDIES. 5/-
COLOSSIAN STUDIES. 5/-
OUTLINES OF CHRISTIAN DOCTRINE. 2/6
VENI CREATOR. 5/-
LETTERS TO MY YOUNGER BRETHREN. 5/-
THE EPISTLE TO THE ROMANS. 7/6

MUIR (Rev. PEARSON McADAM, D.D.)

MODERN SUBSTITUTES FOR CHRISTIANITY. 6/-

MUIR (Rev. WILLIAM, M.A., B.D., B.L.)

CHRISTIANITY AND LABOUR. 6/-

NEW HISTORY OF METHODISM, A
Edited by W. J. Townsend, D.D., H. B. Workman, M.A., D.Lit., and George Eayrs, F.R.Hist.S. In two large volumes. Profusely illustrated. 30/-

NICOLL (Sir W. ROBERTSON, M.A. LL.D.,

THE EXPOSITOR'S DICTIONARY OF TEXTS.
Edited by the Rev. Sir W. Robertson Nicoll, LL.D. and Jane T. Stoddart, with the co-operation of the Rev. James Moffatt, D.D. Complete in two volumes. 25/- net each. (See page 6.,

THE EXPOSITOR'S GREEK TESTAMENT.
Edited by the Rev. Sir W. Robertson Nicoll, LL.D. Complete in five volumes. £3 15/- net the set; single volumes 28/-; any two volumes 30/- net. (See page 6.)

THE EXPOSITOR'S BIBLE.
Edited by the Rev. Sir W. Robertson Nicoll, LL.D. Series I. to VII. of six volumes each, 24/- net the set; Series VIII. of seven volumes, 28/- net the set; single volumes 7/6. (See page 5.)

SUNDAY EVENING. 5/- net.
THE LAMP OF SACRIFICE 6/-
THE CHURCH'S ONE FOUNDATION : Christ and Recent Criticism. 1/6 net; leather, 2/6 net.
THE KEY OF THE GRAVE. 1/6 net; leather, 2/6 net.
THE LAMB OF GOD : Expositions in the Writings of St. John. 1/6 net; leather, 2/6 net.
THE GARDEN OF NUTS : Mystical Expositions. Cloth 2/- net. Leather 2/6 net.
THE RETURN TO THE CROSS. 1/6 net; leather, 2/6 net.
TEN MINUTE SERMONS. 1/6 net; leather, 2/6 net.
THE SEVEN WORDS FROM THE CROSS. Cloth, 1/- net.
SONGS OF REST.
Cloth 5/- in two vols., in case, 2/6; in one vol., leather, 2/6 net; series I. and II., 1/6 each.
SUNDAY AFTERNOON VERSES. 3/6
MY FATHER. With portraits. 1/-
THE ROUND OF THE CLOCK 6/-
A BOOK OF FAMILY WORSHIP. 5/-
IAN MACLAREN. Life of Rev. John Watson, D.D. With photogravure portrait. 6/-

Hodder & Stoughton, Publishers, Warwick Sq., London, E.C.

THEOLOGICAL AND RELIGIOUS LITERATURE

OMAN (Rev. JOHN, M.A., B.D., D.Phil.)
THE CHURCH AND THE DIVINE ORDER. 6/-
VISION AND AUTHORITY; or The Throne of St. Peter. 7/6
THE PROBLEM OF FAITH AND FREEDOM IN THE LAST TWO CENTURIES. 10/6

ORR (Rev. Professor JAMES, M.A. D.D.)
THE RITSCHLIAN THEOLOGY AND THE EVANGELICAL FAITH. 2/6
NEGLECTED FACTORS IN THE EARLY HISTORY OF CHRISTIANITY. 3/6
THE PROGRESS OF DOGMA. 7/6
GOD'S IMAGE IN MAN AND ITS DEFACEMENT IN THE LIGHT OF MODERN DENIALS. 6/-
THE EARLY CHURCH : ITS HISTORY AND LITERATURE. 1/- net.
THE VIRGIN BIRTH OF CHRIST. 6/-
THE RESURRECTION OF CHRIST. 6/-
SIN AS A PROBLEM OF TO-DAY. 6/-
THE FAITH OF A MODERN CHRISTIAN. 5/-

OTTMAN (Rev. FORD C., D.D.)
GOD'S OATH. A Study of an Unfulfilled Promise to David. 5/- net.

PARKER (JOSEPH, D.D.)
THE APOSTOLIC LIFE, as delineated in the Acts of the Apostles. In three volumes. 8/- each.
TYNE CHYLDE, my Life and Ministry. 7/6
THE PEOPLE'S BIBLE. Complete in twenty-five volumes. Cheap edition, 6/- each.
THE PULPIT BIBLE. 42/- net.
ST. PAUL'S EPISTLES TO THE COLOSSIANS AND THESSALONIANS. 5/-
ST. PAUL'S EPISTLE TO THE EPHESIANS. 5/-

PATON (JOHN G., D.D.)
AN AUTOBIOGRAPHY. 6/-; popular edition, 6d.
LATER YEARS AND FAREWELL. Illustrated, 3/6

PATON (FRANK H. L., B.D.)
THE TRIUMPH OF THE GOSPEL IN THE NEW HEBRIDES. 3/6

PEAKE (Prof. A. S., D.D.)
A GUIDE TO BIBLICAL STUDY. With an introduction by the Rev. A. M. Fairbairn, D.D. 3/6
HEROES AND MARTYRS OF FAITH. 5/-

PEMBER (G. H., M.A.)
EARTH'S EARLIEST AGES, and their Connection with Spiritualism and Theosophy. 7/6
THE GREAT PROPHECIES OF THE CENTURIES CONCERNING ISRAEL AND THE GENTILES 7/6
THE GREAT PROPHECIES OF THE CENTURIES CONCERNING THE CHURCH. 7/6

PIERSON (A. T., D.D.)
THE KEY WORDS OF THE BIBLE Purple cloth, 2/- net; leather, 2/6 net.

PIGOU (The Very Rev. FRANCIS. D.D.)
THE ACTS OF THE HOLY GHOST 6/-

PURPLE LEATHER LIBRARY (THE) Purple leather, 2/6 net; Boards, 1/6 net. each.
THE RETURN TO THE CROSS. Sir W. Robertson Nicoll, M.A., LL.D.
TEN MINUTE SERMONS. Sir W. Robertson Nicoll, M.A., LL.D.
THE LAMB OF GOD. Sir W. Robertson Nicoll, M.A., LL.D.
THE KEY OF THE GRAVE. Sir W. Robertson Nicoll, M.A., LL.D.
THE CHURCH'S ONE FOUNDATION Sir W. Robertson Nicoll, M.A., LL.D.
STUDIES IN THE TEACHING OF OUR LORD. Rev. Prof. H. B. Swete, D.D.

Hodder & Stoughton, Publishers, Warwick Sq., London, E.C.

THEOLOGICAL AND RELIGIOUS LITERATURE

PURPLE LEATHER LIBRARY.—contd.

THE COMMUNION TABLE.
Rev. L. Maclean Watt, B.D.

CHRIST MYSTICAL.
Joseph Hall, D.D.

IN CHRIST.   A. J. Gordon, D.D.

THE FOUR MEN.
Prof. James Stalker, D.D.

MEMORANDA SACRA.
Prof. J. Rendel Harris.

RUYSBROECK AND THE MYSTICS
Maurice Maeterlinck.

WEEKDAY RELIGION
J. R. Miller, D.D.

LETTERS ON LIFE. Claudius Clear.

MARGARET OGILVY. J. M. Barrie.

THE PRAYER THAT TEACHES TO
PRAY.   Marcus Dods, D.D.

THE TWOFOLD LIFE.
A. J. Gordon, D.D.

W. V., HER BOOK. William Canton.

RAINY (Rev. Principal ROBERT, D.D.)

THE EPISTLE TO THE PHILIP-
PIANS.   7/6

**RAMSAY (Sir W. M., D.C.L., LL.D.,
D.D.)**

THE HISTORICAL VALUE OF
THE ACTS OF THE APOSTLES.
12/-

THE FIRST CHRISTIAN CEN-
TURY.   2/6 net.

THE CHURCH IN THE ROMAN
EMPIRE, BEFORE A.D. 170.
With maps and illustrations, 12/-

ST. PAUL THE TRAVELLER AND
THE ROMAN CITIZEN.   10/6

WAS CHRIST BORN AT BETHLE-
HEM?   5/-

A HISTORICAL COMMENTARY ON
ST. PAUL'S EPISTLE TO THE
GALATIANS.   With maps, 12/-

THE EDUCATION OF CHRIST.
Purple cloth, 2/- net; leather, 2/6 net.

LETTERS TO THE SEVEN CHUR-
CHES OF ASIA.   Illustrated, 12/-

PAULINE, AND OTHER STUDIES.
12/-

THE CITIES OF ST. PAUL.
Illustrated, 12/-

LUKE THE PHYSICIAN.   12/-

RAMSAY (Sir W. M.)—contd.

PICTURES OF THE APOSTOLIC
CHURCH.   6/-

STUDIES IN THE HISTORY AND
ART OF THE EASTERN PRO-
VINCES OF THE ROMAN EM-
PIRE.   20/- net.

THE THOUSAND AND ONE
CHURCHES. Illustrated, 20/- net.

REID (Prof. H. M. B., D.D.)

THE PROFESSOR'S WALLET.   6/-

ROBERTSON (Prof. A. T., A.M., D.D.)

A SHORT GRAMMAR OF THE
GREEK NEW TESTAMENT.
6/- net.

EPOCHS IN THE LIFE OF JESUS.
2/6 net.

RYDER (Rev. Canon A. R., B.D.)

THE PRIESTHOOD OF THE
LAITY.   6/-

RYLE (Right Reverend J. C., D.D.)

EXPOSITORY THOUGHTS ON
THE GOSPELS. Seven volumes.
4/- each.

SABATIER (PAUL)

THE LIFE OF ST. FRANCIS
D'ASSISI.   7/6

SABATIER (M. A.)

THE APOSTLE PAUL : A Sketch of
the Development of his Doctrine.
7/6

SABATIER (AUGUSTE)

OUTLINES OF A PHILOSOPHY OF
RELIGION.   7/6

SANKEY (IRA D.)

MY LIFE AND SACRED SONGS.
Introduction by the late Theodore
L. Cuyler, D.D.   1/-

SCHOFIELD (A. T., M.D.)

STUDIES IN THE HIGHEST
THOUGHT.   3/6

THE KNOWLEDGE OF GOD.   3/6

SCLATER (Rev. J. R. P., M.A.)

THE ENTERPRISE OF LIFE.
Fifty-two Addresses to Young Men.
5/- net.

Hodder & Stoughton, Publishers, Warwick Sq., London, E.C.

THEOLOGICAL AND RELIGIOUS LITERATURE

SCOTT (Rev. A. BOYD, M.A., B.D.)
BRANCHES OF THE CROSS. 6/-

SCOTT (Rev. C. ANDERSON, M.A.)
EVANGELICAL DOCTRINE, BIBLE
TRUTH. 1/- net.

SELBIE (Rev. Principal W. B., M.A.)
THE HISTORY AND WITNESS OF
EVANGELICAL CHRISTIANITY.
6/-
ASPECTS OF CHRIST. 6/-
THE SERVANT OF GOD. 6/-

SELBY (Rev. T. G.)
THE UNHEEDING GOD, and other
Sermons. 6/-
THE GOD OF THE FRAIL, and
other Sermons. 6/-
THE STRENUOUS GOSPEL. 6/-

SELWYN (Rev. Canon E. C., D.D.)
ORACLES IN THE NEW TESTA-
MENT. 10/6 net.

SHEPHERD (Rev. AMBROSE, D.D.)
THE GOSPEL AND SOCIAL QUES-
TIONS. 2/6
MEN IN THE MAKING. 3/6
BIBLE STUDIES IN LIVING SUB-
JECTS. 3/6 net.

SIMPSON (Rev. P. CARNEGIE, D.D.)
THE FACT OF CHRIST. 3/6
Popular edition, 1/- net.
THE SITE OF UNION. 6d.
LOVE NEVER FAILETH. 5/-
THE LIFE OF PRINCIPAL RAINY.
New edition. 7/6

SIMPSON (Rev. Canon J. G., M.A., D.D.)
THE SPIRIT AND THE BRIDE. 6/-
CHRISTIAN IDEALS. 6/-
CHRISTUS CRUCIFIXUS. 6/-

SIMPSON (Prof. J. Y., M.A., D.Sc.)
THE SPIRITUAL INTERPRETA-
TION OF NATURE. 6/-

SMITH (Rev. Professor DAVID, M.A., D.D.)
CHRISTIAN COUNSEL. 5/-
THE DAYS OF HIS FLESH.
10/6 net.
THE PILGRIM'S HOSPICE. 3/6
A LEGEND OF BETHLEHEM.
1/- net.
A LEGEND OF JERUSALEM.
1/- net.
MAN'S NEED OF GOD. 6/-
THE FEAST OF THE COVENANT.
A new and revised edition of Prof.
David Smith's book on the Holy
Communion. 3/6

SMITH (Principal GEORGE ADAM, D.D., LL.D.)
THE BOOK OF ISAIAH.
Two vols., 7/6 each.
MODERN CRITICISM AND
PREACHING OF THE OLD
TESTAMENT 6/-
THE HISTORICAL GEOGRAPHY
OF THE HOLY LAND. 15/-
THE BOOKS OF THE TWELVE
PROPHETS. Two vols., 7/6 each.
FOUR PSALMS. 1/- net.
THE FORGIVENESS OF SINS, and
other Sermons. 6/-
JERUSALEM. Two vols., 24/- net.
THE LIFE OF HENRY DRUM-
MOND, F.R.S.E. 3/6

SMYTH (Rev. J. PATERSON, B.D., LL.D., D.C.L.)
THE GOSPEL OF THE HERE-
AFTER. 2/6 net.

SMYTH (NEWMAN, D.D.)
PASSING PROTESTANTISM AND
COMING CATHOLICISM. 5/-

STALKER (Rev. Professor JAMES, M.A., D.D.)
IMAGO CHRISTI : The Example of
Jesus Christ. 5/-
THE PREACHER AND HIS
MODELS. 5/-
THE FOUR MEN.
1/6 net; leather, 2/6 net.

Hodder & Stoughton, Publishers, Warwick Sq., London, E.C.

THEOLOGICAL AND RELIGIOUS LITERATURE

STALKER (Rev. J.)—contd.
THE TRIAL AND DEATH OF JESUS CHRIST.   5/-
THE CHRISTOLOGY OF JESUS.   6/-
THE SEVEN DEADLY SINS.   1/- net.
THE SEVEN CARDINAL VIRTUES   1/- net.
JOHN KNOX: HIS IDEAS AND IDEALS.   3/6
THE ATONEMENT.   2/6
THE ETHIC OF JESUS ACCORD-ING TO THE SYNOPTIC GOS-PELS.   7/6

STEVEN (Rev. GEORGE, B.A.)
THE PSYCHOLOGY OF THE CHRISTIAN SOUL.   6/-

STOKES (Rev. Prof. G. T.)
THE ACTS OF THE APOSTLES. Two vols.   7/6 each.

STOUGHTON (JOHN, D.D.)
LIGHTS AND SHADOWS OF CHURCH LIFE.   6/-
HISTORY OF RELIGION IN ENG-LAND, from the opening of the Long Parliament to the end of the Eighteenth Century. Eight vols., £3 the set; single vols., 7/6.
RECOLLECTIONS OF A LONG LIFE.   6/-
THE DAILY PRAYER BOOK, for the use of Families.   3/6
JOHN STOUGHTON, D.D. (By his Daughter). With photogravure por-trait.   3/6

STREATFEILD (Rev. G. S., M.A.)
THE SELF-INTERPRETATION OF JESUS CHRIST.   5/-

STRONG (JAMES, LL.D.)
THE EXHAUSTIVE CONCORD-ANCE TO THE BIBLE.   20/- net.

SWETE (Prof. H. B., D.D.)
STUDIES IN THE TEACHING OF OUR LORD.
1/6 net; leather, 2/6 net.

SWINSTEAD (Rev. J. HOWARD, M.A.)
IN A WONDERFUL ORDER: A Study of Angels.   2/6 net.

TAIT (Rev. ARTHUR J., M.A.)
CHRIST AND THE NATIONS.   5/-

TAYLOR (Rev. W. M., D.D.)
THE PARABLES OF OUR SAVIOUR EXPOUNDED AND ILLUSTRA-TED.   7/6
THE MIRACLES OF OUR SAVIOUR EXPOUNDED AND ILLUSTRA-TED.   7/6

THEOLOGICAL EDUCATOR (THE)
Edited by the Rev. Sir W. Robertson Nicoll, M.A., LL.D.   2/6 each.
A MANUAL OF CHRISTIAN EVI-DENCES. Rev. Prebendary Row, M.A., D.D.
A HEBREW GRAMMAR. Rev. W Lowe, M.A.
MANUAL OF CHURCH HISTORY. Rev. A. C. Jennings, M.A. Two volumes.
EXPOSITION OF THE APOSTLES' CREED. Rev. J. E. Yonge, M.A.
THE PRAYER BOOK. Rev. Charles Hole, B.A.
OUTLINES OF CHRISTIAN DOC-TRINE. Rt. Rev. H. G. C. Moule, D.D., Lord Bishop of Durham.
AN INTRODUCTION TO THE OLD TESTAMENT. Rev. C. H. H. Wright, D.D.
THE THEOLOGY OF THE OLD TESTAMENT. Rev. Prof. W. H. Bennett, M.A., D.D., D.Litt.
THE THEOLOGY OF THE NEW TESTAMENT. Rev. Prof. W. F. Adeney. M.A.

Hodder & Stoughton, Publishers, Warwick Sq., London, E.C.

THEOLOGICAL AND RELIGIOUS LITERATURE

THEOLOGICAL EDUCATOR.—contd.

AN INTRODUCTION TO THE TEXTUAL CRITICISM OF THE NEW TESTAMENT. Rev. Prof. B. B. Warfield, D.D.

AN INTRODUCTION TO THE NEW TESTAMENT. Rev. Principal Marcus Dods, D.D.

THE LANGUAGE OF THE NEW TESTAMENT. Rev. W. H. Simcox, M.A.

THE WRITERS OF THE NEW TESTAMENT : Their Style and Characteristics. Rev. W. H. Simcox, M.A.

EVOLUTION AND CHRISTIANITY. Rev. Prof. James Iverach, D.D.

THE RITSCHLIAN THEOLOGY AND THE EVANGELICAL FAITH Rev. Prof. James Orr, M.A., D.D.

TESKEY (A. M.)

A LITTLE CHILD SHALL LEAD THEM. Illustrated in colour. 1/- net.

THOMAS (Rev. JOHN, M.A.)

THE MYSTERIES OF GRACE. 6/-

THOMAS (Rev. Principal W. H. GRIFFITH, D.D.)

THE CATHOLIC FAITH.
Cloth, 2/-; paper, 1/- net.

THE WORK OF THE MINISTRY.
6/- net.

VAN DYKE (HENRY, D.D., LL.D.)

THE GOSPEL FOR A WORLD OF SIN. 5/-

THE GOSPEL FOR AN AGE OF DOUBT. 5/-

MANHOOD, FAITH AND COURAGE. 5/-

IDEALS AND APPLICATIONS.
3/6 net.

OUT OF DOORS IN THE HOLY LAND. Illustrated in colour, 6/- net

VAUGHAN (Rev. JAMES)

FIFTY-TWO SERMONS TO CHILDREN. 5/- net.

WARFIELD (Rev. Prof. B. B., D.D.)

AN INTRODUCTION TO THE TEXTUAL CRITICISM OF THE NEW TESTAMENT. 2/6

WATSON (JOHN, M.A., D.D.)

THE DOCTRINES OF GRACE. 6/-

THE MIND OF THE MASTER. 6/-

THE UPPER ROOM. 1/- net.

THE POTTER'S WHEEL. 3/6

THE LIFE OF THE MASTER. 6/-

THE INSPIRATION OF OUR FAITH. 6/-

GOD'S MESSAGE TO THE HUMAN SOUL. 5/- net.

THE SCOT OF THE EIGHTEENTH CENTURY. 5/-

RESPECTABLE SINS. 3/6

IAN MACLAREN. Life of the Rev. John Watson, D.D. By the Rev. Sir W Robertson Nicoll, LL.D. With photogravure portrait. 6/-

WATSON (R. A., D.D.)

THE BOOK OF JOB. 7/6

JUDGES AND RUTH. 7/6

THE BOOK OF NUMBERS. 7/6

WATSON (Rev. DAVID)

PERFECT WOMANHOOD. 3/6

SOCIAL ADVANCE. 5/-

WATT (Rev. L. MACLEAN, B.D.)

THE COMMUNION TABLE.
Cloth, 2/- net; leather, 2/6 net.

EDRAGIL, 1745. 3/6

MORAN OF KILDALLY. 6/-

IN POETS' CORNER. 3/6

WELLS (Rev. JAMES, M.A., D.D.)

RESCUERS AND RESCUED. 3/6

CHRIST IN THE PRESENT AGE. 3/6

THE LIFE OF J. HOOD WILSON, D.D. 7/6

THE LIFE OF JAMES STEWART OF LOVEDALE. With portrait and illustrations. 2/6

Hodder & Stoughton, Publishers, Warwick Sq., London, E.C.

THEOLOGICAL AND RELIGIOUS LITERATURE

WENDLAND (Professor J.)
MIRACLES AND CHRISTIANITY. Edited by Professor H. R. Mackintosh, D.D.   6/-

WENYON (Rev. CHARLES, M.D.)
THE CREATION STORY IN THE LIGHT OF TO-DAY.   3/6

WHYTE (ALEXANDER, D.D.)
CHARACTERS AND CHARACTER- ISTICS OF WILLIAM LAW, Non- juror and Mystic.   3/6
THE FOUR TEMPERAMENTS.   1/- net.

WILLIAMS (J. E. HODDER)
THE LIFE OF SIR GEORGE WIL- LIAMS.   Illustrated, 6/-
      Popular edition, 1/- net.

WELLS (Rev. JAMES, D.D.)
THE LIFE OF JAMES STEWART OF LOVEDALE.
      Illustrated, 5/- net.

WORCESTER (Rev. ELWOOD, D.D., Ph.D.)
THE LIVING WORD.   6/-

YOUNG (Rev. DINSDALE T.)
UNFAMILIAR TEXTS.   3/6
THE CRIMSON BOOK.   3/6
PETER MACKENZIE AS I KNEW HIM.   2/6
THE ENTHUSIASM OF GOD.   3/6
MESSAGES FOR HOME AND LIFE   3/6
THE GOSPEL OF THE LEFT HAND.   3/6
IN SILVER CHAINS.   3/6

Hodder & Stoughton, Publishers, Warwick Sq., London. E.C.